Revised Edition.

First published in 2024 by Bitza Books

Previously published by Bitza Books under the title The Churchfield Murder ©2022

bitzabooks.co.uk

© John Brookland, 2024

Ebook ISBN: 9781068645020

Print ISBN: 9781068645037

The moral right of John Brookland to be identified as the author has been asserted in accordance with the Copyright, Designs and Patents Act, 1988

All rights reserved. No part of this book may be reprinted or reproduced or utilised in any form or by any electric, mechanical or other means now known, or hereafter invented, including photocopying and recoding, or in any information storage or retrieval system, without permission in writing from the publisher.

A CIP catalogue record for this book is available from the British Library.

Every effort has been made to fulfil requirements regarding reproducing copyright material. The author will be glad to rectify any omissions at the earliest opportunity. All the persons and places mentioned in the book are real, as is all of the testimony but some of the dialogue and scenes are fictionalised to make the story understandable.

With thanks to my partner Debbie for her
help in producing my books.

The Edwardian Detective Edwin Fowle Series
The Tonbridge Outrage
The Tenterden Murder
Coming Soon
Casebook of a Real Edwardian Detective
The Sevenoaks Tragedy

THE TENTERDEN MURDER

An Edwardian Murder Most Brutal

John Brookland

BritzaBooks

Table of Contents

PROLOGUE

The town of Tenterden is situated in the English County of Kent nestled in an area known as the Garden of England. It has been famous for several centuries for its charm and scenic high street. In Victorian and Edwardian times it was a popular destination for outings by charabancs from nearby large towns such as Ashford and Maidstone and for other tourists particularly in the spring and summer; a tradition that continues today. It boasted many hostelries who made a good living out of these visitors. It was a typical small market town surrounded by hop fields and orchards and was a centre of sheep farming making it a bustling place.

A mile outside of Tenterden is a small hamlet named St. Michaels which in 1905 was home to just 632 souls. It was separated from the town by open fields and a large country estate called Homewood. It consisted mainly of a collection of terraced farm workers and labourers' cottages served by one tavern, a bakery, a blacksmith, a village school and a church on the hill overlooking it. It also had a small halt on a new railway line recently opened. It was surrounded by woodland, orchards, hop fields and meadows with dirt tracks for roads and no street lighting. Although many passed through on their way to Tenterden, few if any stopped or even noticed the community

This was to rudely change on a warm June morning in 1905 when a brutally murdered man was found in a meadow adjacent to the church known locally as Churchfield, which is now buried under a housing development. Today it is difficult to distinguish where St. Michaels ends, and the town begins as the space between has disappeared under development over the decades. There is nothing to indicate the spot where a "strange and ghastly" bloody murder took place.

The local community usually experienced crimes such as poaching, petty burglary, sheep rustling, and drunkenness and so rural policing was a relatively laid-back affair with just the odd bobby or two

1

wandering the area on foot and known to all the residents. It was for the most part a convivial atmosphere whereby the local "villains" were well known to the police and crime detection was a bit of a game. Because of this, the Tenterden police department consisted of just a sergeant and three constables based in a small corner building in the centre of the high street in front of St. Mildreds Church. But it did boast a couple of cells and a small court room on the first floor.

Serious crimes such as murder were few and far between and so when the body was found it came as quite a shock to both the residents and the police. Rural constables had little or no training in investigating such incidents and were hampered by the lack of the technological and forensic assets that modern policing enjoy. There was no thought of approaching a crime scene "using the path of least common approach" or "bagging evidence" in order to preserve it as there is today. It was early days in the investigation of serious crime and with the exception of Scotland Yard in London most police forces had no specialised detective departments until the late 1800s. Finger printing was only just being trialled in some cities, CCTV and DNA testing was nearly a century in the future. There was not even a test to distinguish between human and animal blood. Therefore, most convictions were gained by collecting circumstantial evidence and this lack of corroborative forensics led to many accused persons being wrongly convicted on just witness testimony. The legal process was also convoluted with inquest and investigative magistrate hearings, grand juries and assize courts.

The availability of adequate communication and transport was also an issue. The only means of distance transport available was by horseback, train or hired cab and there were only twenty police bicycles in the whole of the County of Kent, so officers completed their beat on foot. Telephones were few and far between and a luxury of the rich; and messages had to be passed by electric telegram, post or runner. So, when solving serious crime, the police were always handicapped.

It was in this context that Divisional Superintendent Thomas Fowle, head of the Cranbrook Division, was faced in solving the murder. Kent was divided into twelve divisions each headed by a superintendent, the highest rank at the time apart from the Chief Constable and his deputy. Kent police had the prescience in 1896 to inaugurate a small detective department at its Wrens Cross headquarters in Maidstone. Once established it proved to be a very productive and successful unit even though it only consisted of just a sergeant and three constables responsible for the whole County. It was an early equivalent of the Flying Squad or Sweeney. It became protocol for these superintendents to immediately refer high profile complex cases requiring specialist investigation to them and this is exactly what Thomas Fowle did. The detectives were nominally independent only answerable to the Chief Constable, but they worked closely with whatever area superintendent they happened to be working in reporting to him every day and "working up" a case for the superintendent to act on.

Heading the department was a much respected and renowned newly promoted officer in the form of First-Class Detective Sergeant Edwin Fowle who had been one of first three detective constables. He happened to be the son of Thomas and this father and son combination was about to work on the case together. Edwin had been in charge for five years and had gained much respect from his colleagues and superiors for his excellent investigative work. He had a great sense of duty, was a driven man, who was religious and was a stickler for correct police procedure. He was to have an unrivalled record of success as a detective in the Force and is the protagonist in the tale.

What follows is a factual narrative of a brutal murder that occurred in the hamlet of St. Michaels, Tenterden, Kent, in 1905 and describes the investigation and events that took place on the day of the murder and subsequently between Saturday 17 June and the 1 August 1905 from the perspective of all those involved. Although the murder took place in St Michaels it was dubbed by the press as the "Tenterden Murder," mainly because they knew their readers would not recognise the village. All the persons and places mentioned are real, as is all of the testimony but some of the dialogue and scenes are fictionalised to make the story understandable.

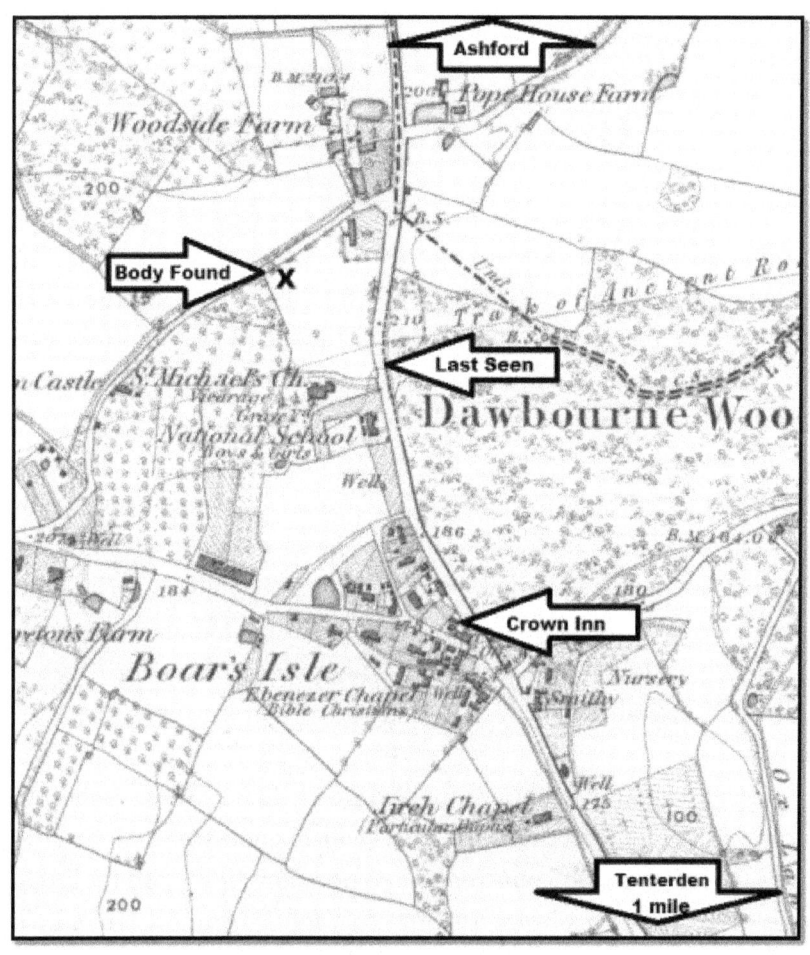

St Michaels, Tenterden. Map of Locations involved with the murder.

1 :

Dreams of a Better Life

In the tiny Saharan desert village of Omar in Algeria surrounded by barren ground and herds of goats an extended family lived who dreamed of a better life. They had the nerve and confidence to envisage traveling to Europe to find it. The instigator of this venture was a 38-year-old Hadj ou Iddir a rather diminutive man only 5 feet seven inches tall and of slim build with black curly hair and a well-manicured pencil moustache. He wore the traditional clothing of the period including a red fez with a tassel. He was an experienced trader and wanted to put his talents to better use and more profit. He had heard from many people that there were lucrative possibilities for itinerant traders like themselves in Europe leading to permanent residency in a country. After much discussion and persuasion he managed to convince several members of his family to join him in a venture to migrate.

They consisted of his younger brother, Frank Salem, taller and brawnier than his brother with a heavy black moustache curled at the ends who always stood out from his companions. Iddir also took along two of his young nephews: 19-year-old Ferat Mohamed Ben Ali who looked much younger as he was only five feet four inches tall with boyish good looks, dark curly hair and a small moustache. The other nephew was 17-year-old Daka Belkacem of similar looks and build and of a quiet nature. The last of the group was a 17-year-old cousin named Meznow "Oily" Mohammed.

They set off for the city streets of Algiers after much emotional goodbyes to the rest of the clan with Iddir becoming the leader due to his age and business acumen. The group referred to him as "Uncle." They spent some time in Algiers raising money for the trip but in late 1904 they took a boat across the Mediterranean to the port of

Marseille. For the next few months they travelled north through France until they finally arrived at the channel ports, buying and selling mats, tablecloths and trinkets along the way. Hadj ou Iddir managed all the buying of stock and made sure he kept control of the money they obtained. He would then dole out a share of the proceeds to the others as he saw fit. This undoubtably caused some resentment on occasions. They were sometimes excitable and known to argue and gesticulate but mainly in a good-natured way as was their culture.

Despite only speaking French and Arabic, and with a smattering of pidgin English, they decided it might be more lucrative to ply their trade in England and continue their adventure there. They sailed in a ferry to Dover in early 1905 and made their way to London. They were pleasantly surprised at the amount of railway lines which cris-crossed the countryside and were determined to make as much use of them as possible in getting around. Iddir soon hooked up with wholesalers in the Tottenham Court road where they obtained their wares. They spent the winter months trading in London, but with the warmer weather arriving and finding trading in the city difficult they moved their operation to the countryside towns and villages of Kent and East Sussex which were easily accessible.

Their modus operandi was to establish a base in a larger town with a railway for access to London to get their stock. They lived in cheap and sometimes insalubrious lodging houses and taverns and then radiated out on foot, by lifts or on the railway to the smaller hamlets and villages. They were dressed in a mix of traditional and local clothing; some of them maintained their red fez's and red waist sashes and colourful waistcoats. Others a flat cap, a workman's jacket and trousers. Although travelling street hawkers were common in the rural areas and useful, the Algerians must have presented a strange sight and perhaps intimidating. For this reason they rarely went out as a group but split up in two groups or singly to avoid looking like a gang. From all reports they were well behaved, polite and never caused trouble.

Hotels and taverns appeared very willing to accommodate them despite their dishevelled and unusual look. They also appeared to have been welcomed by local residents, who found them a novelty and fascinating, and they soon established a lucrative trade.

In early April 1905 they established a base at a lodging house operated by Mr and Mrs Ferrari at 15 East Hill Passage in Hastings, a large popular seaside town in East Sussex. They rented two rooms and travelled round the local coastal towns and villages. At the end of May, Salem and Meznow moved out and travelled to the village of Robertsbridge, ten miles north of Hastings and on the railway line to London in search of new villages to hawk their goods. Bill Hodges in the signal box at the end of the platform watched them with interest as they alighted from the train and walked up the main street where they attracted a lot of attention from passersby and shopkeepers alike who came to their doors to peer at them. Ted Bashford the butcher was one of them and he leaned on the door frame as they headed up the street turning heads and causing quiet discussions between the women shoppers. They arrived at the Railway Tavern, a rather rough hostelry and entered. They were welcomed by Jane Allen, the landlord's wife, who gave them a room at the back near the kitchen which Salem put to good use while they stayed there.

Each morning they would set off on foot using the tracks and footpaths to other hamlets surrounding the town and occasionally by train to other halts along the line. When possible they hitched lifts on passing waggons otherwise they walked countless miles. They became a familiar sight and began to integrate into the local community. As the evenings became lighter they would go out again to try and catch those that had been at work during the day.

At the beginning of June, Iddir suggested to his two nephews, Belkacem and Ben Ali, who had remained in Hastings, that they had exhausted the trading potential of the area and the three of them should move their base. On the afternoon of Tuesday 13 June they bade goodbye to Mrs Ferrari and travelled by train to the large busy market town of Ashford in Kent twenty-one miles to the northeast. There they took lodgings at the Star Inn on East Hill in the centre of town just a half mile to the station and leading to the High Street. Iddir had sent Belkacem to Robertsbridge to inform the other two of their move and to tell them to join up in Ashford. They booked a room for them at the tavern. While they awaited them they spent the next two days peddling in Ashford, but on Friday 17 June Iddir and Ben Ali, decided to investigate the smaller market town of Tenterden some twelve miles to the south west.

They took a train from Ashford to Headcorn where they changed onto a newly opened branch line that took them to the town. They alighted at the small station at lunchtime and caught the eye of the stationmaster Arthur Taunt who watched them curiously as they left the yard and headed up the track to the High Street. The town was and is still known as the 'Jewel of the Weald' because of its quaintness with wide tree-lined greens, Georgian and Victorian buildings of stucco and traditional tile and weatherboard cottages. It had gas street lighting, an ancient town hall, multiple shops, many hostelries and a new railway which opened in 1905. Life here was more hectic than St Michaels but still languid, and it attracted many tourists which it does to this day.

Again they caused quite a stir during the afternoon as they paraded in their colourful attire up and down the roads. Although shoddily dressed hawkers, handicraft tramps and chapmen were a common sight in rural areas particularly French onion sellers, few foreigners were seen outside the main cities and towns. Itinerant trading was extremely popular with housewives and profitable for the pedlar. Most had the required good humoured doorstep banter and householders found them "picturesque" and charming. Iddir's group attired in their fez hats, checked waistcoats and scarlet waistbands certainly fitted the bill and were watched with fascination by a multitude of local inhabitants who they approached to buy their goods. Everyone mistook them for being Turkish because of their attire.

That afternoon Iddir and Ben Ali walked east along Tenterden High Street past all the shops until they reached houses where they could begin offering their colourful mats, cheap jewellery, linens and other "gimcrackery." They kept on walking, resting on convenient benches when tired, and eventually arrived in the hamlet of St. Michaels. Trade was good and they appeared satisfied and happy.

*

The hamlet of St Michaels on a warm June day was a relatively idyllic place to live. It was a community where everyone knew each other, peaceful with little crime and most people were content with their lot. The housewives got on with their work, taking the children the short distance to the school adjacent to the church, doing their morning chores and visiting the bakery. Later they might walk the mile into Tenterden for their main shop where they were spoilt for shopping opportunities. Husbands, sons and boyfriends would be hard at work in the fields, orchards, woods and hop fields that surrounded the hamlet or working in Tenterden in the brewery, shops and small factories. Older folk would be sitting on the bench outside the Crown Inn the only tavern smoking their pipes.

Many residents had their doors knocked by the strange pair that afternoon. The housewives were accosted as they put their washing out or were chatting to their neighbours while the men in the fields leaned on their tools for a few seconds to watch them walk by laden with their bundles. Sarah Appleyard was the wife of the St Michaels schoolmaster and lived with her husband in the school house. She happened to be looking out her front window at about 4pm and spotted two strange swarthy men, one older with a tiny moustache and the other only a young lad, both wearing red fez's walking down the road from the direction of the church. They were quite a sight and not the usual passerby. At first she thought they were vagabonds as they were carrying large bundles but as they got nearer decided they must be hawkers. She aware there were many door-to-door foreign sellers wandering the countryside who could be a nuisance sometimes and she guessed they would be soon walking up to her front door. But surprisingly they sauntered passed her gate and she noticed their red waist sashes. She immediately thought them to be Turkish. They headed in the direction of the main village, and she was relieved that she would not have to turn them away.

Just down the road was an area of allotments and 28-year-old farm labourer William Roberts, who lived in Yew Tree cottages, was tending his plot helped by a friend, It bordered the main road and just after 4pm they too saw Iddir and Ben Ali approaching and his friend shouted out good humouredly, "Here comes the Russians," and chuckled. The two hawkers took it in good spirit, nodded and gave them a smile and continued through the hamlet offering their wares to anyone they passed and headed back to Tenterden.

18-year-old Gwendoline Cole, a school teacher, lived at 2 Beacon Oak Road a few hundred yards from the high street and was going into town on an errand at 5pm and came across Iddir and Ben Ali resting on a bench situated on the main road into town at the bottom of her road. They called out to her asking if she wanted to buy any jewellery. Intrigued she went over to them and chatted while they laid out the gimcrackery which she perused. She decided not to buy anything much to their disappointment as she recognised it as cheap quality. After running a few errands she headed home at about 6pm and saw the older pedlar still sitting on the bench. As she turned up Beacon Oak Road heading for her house she noticed the other young man coming out of a copse that bordered the opposite side of the road and coming towards her. He was holding something behind his back, but she didn't take much notice of him believing he had been in there to relieve himself. She watched him join his friend.

Meanwhile in Robertsbridge, Edward Bashford the butcher was standing in the shop doorway that afternoon greeting people as they went by and watched a young foreigner wearing a red sash who he hadn't seen before walk up from the station. He was well aware that two hawkers were lodging at the tavern and immediately thought that this young fellow might be connected to them. He had forged a relationship with the two as they often came into his shop to buy meat to cook meals in the tavern kitchen and he knew them as Salem and Oily. He watched as the lad nervously walked past him towards the Railway Inn and go in. A few minutes later he came out again looking concerned and later he saw him heading back to the station.

*

Sarah Appleyard had a meeting in Tenterden that evening and as she walked into town she spotted the same two hawkers sitting on the bench as she passed by on the other side of the road at just before 8pm. Twenty minutes later while in town she saw the young hawker on his own in the High Street. On her way home at about 10.45pm she came across the older one near the Crown Inn in St. Michaels heading towards Tenterden. She thought it was rather late for them to be out and about and wondered where they might be staying, but guessed they must be sleeping rough. She couldn't believe how many times she had bumped into them that day.

It was common for such hawkers to ply their trade in pubs in the evenings. Most landlords had no problem with them, other less understanding ones often ejected them. The Eight Bells public house in the centre of Tenterden opposite the church a popular and lively drinking house but like many English pubs has met its demise. It was just a matter of yards from the police station standing on the corner of Church road which made it less raucous than some others. It attracted a mix of thirsty labourers and townsfolk after a hard day's work. That Friday evening was no different and it was packed. Someone was playing on the piano in the corner adding background to the laughing and dart playing. William Stace, the barman was happy with having a packed bar and entering into the banter taking place. It helped pass the time. At about 8.30pm the door opened, and two swarthy "foreigners" walked in. One was the young lad Ben Ali carrying a heavy bundle over his shoulder. His companion was not the older Iddir, but Salem his brother. Being of heavier build and stature, with a bushy moustache turned up at the ends he made quite an entrance.

The room went incredibly quiet while the customers took in the sight, and they were quickly recognised as hawkers. Salem and Ben Ali went up to the bar and all eyes followed them. They bought a drink, but for some strange reason made no attempt to sell their wares. The bar soon returned to its convivial atmosphere, but an interested and wary eye was kept on them as many present had never come into contact with such people. Ben Ali and Salem sheepishly sat in a corner where they were seen to be chatting intensely but as they were obviously feeling uncomfortable they left after only ten minutes having drunk their beer.

The two hawkers then walked across the High Street to the Woolpack Inn, a coaching house next to the church and beside the Town Hall. They went in but after a while were spotted by the 38-year-old landlord Albert Bishop when he entered the bar from the back. He made his way to them and was asked if he wanted to buy anything. Albert was rather short with them and later said, 'they asked me twice if I wanted to buy anything and I said I didn't want them in there and threw them out.' At about 10.45pm Ben Ali was seen back in the Eight Bells where he downed another beer leaving at 11pm, but there was no sign of Salem.

Back in St Michaels William Roberts who had seen Iddir earlier in the afternoon, was heading to the Crown Inn at about 8pm on his way back from his allotment when he saw Iddir drinking from the village pump outside. Inside the Crown Inn, William Reeves, the landlord was also having a busy evening. The pub was the hub of the community and had been in the hands of his family for decades. William knew everybody and everybody knew him. His pub was always busy in the evenings and that Friday was no different. He had a group of regulars numbering some fourteen all in good spirits. There was the sound of dominoes being played and a lot of laughing and jeering as men joked and others played darts in the corner. It was a boisterous atmosphere, but about 8.30pm the door opened and in walked a small man with a pencil moustache and wearing a red fez cap carrying a large bundle which immediately silenced the room.

'Hello, what we got 'ere then?' called one of the drinkers and everyone turned to look. The man stood in the doorway and sheepishly smiled at the room, someone laughed at the sight of him, and the noise and banter soon resumed, but they all continued to stare fascinated by the newcomer. Iddir shuffled up to the bar and asked William, 'Me sell. O.K?'

William allowed him to work the room showing his table cloths, mats and small trinkets and jewellery. The customers embraced the presence of the man and made him the butt of good-natured joking, but Iddir was familiar with such attention and played on it by wearing cultural attire. It was part and parcel of his trade. He was a skilled seller and very soon was finding business as many bought off him, although he was "bartered down to just 4 shillings a mat." He made over two pounds in the pub.

One of his customers was William Milton, the local baker who lived opposite and came in late on when the hawker was almost sold out. After considerable haggling he bought the last set of table cloths for his wife for six shillings and sixpence. Feeling he had done well on the deal William offered to buy Iddir a drink, but the man declined saying 'me no drink,' which William took to mean he was teetotal. But because Iddir felt he had been treated so well and was in a cheerful mood having done so much business, he generously bought a round for all those who had purchased from him. This obviously resulted in raucous cheers from the locals and Iddir left the pub about 10.30pm a firm friend.

George Bassett, a local livestock drover, was also there enjoying the entertainment provided by this unexpected exotic foreign visitor and was one of those waving him off. He finished his drink and left the pub at about 11pm and trudged towards his cottage at 3 Silver Hill opposite the Fat Ox pub, a half mile towards Tenterden on the main road. As he approached his home he met Iddir again heading back towards St Michaels but this time he had a similarly dressed companion with him who was young and a few inches shorter than him. His companion was carrying a thick piece of wood which "he kept twiddling about" behind his back. This made George a bit wary of the young one, but he bade them a friendly good night and they spoke to him.

'We need place to sleep,' said Iddir.

'Bit late isn't it to find lodging?' replied George keeping one eye on the stick and the other on Iddir.

'Yes we need lodging,' repeated Iddir.

'Well, there's a couple of cottages down the road there sometimes takes people in,' said George. He was going to show them to the cottages and help them but felt a little unsafe about the stick, so he just said goodnight and watched the two walking towards St Michaels in the moonlight.

Back at the Eight Bells a labourer named William Curtis who had been sitting at the bar when Salem and Ben Ali first came in, and like everyone else had watched them with great interest until they had left. Having finished his drink, William continued his regular pub crawl by walking across the road and down past the Town Hall to one of his other favourite haunts, the New Inn; another drinking house that hasn't survived. Having supped a couple more "mild's," he left at 11pm and started the long walk back to his home in St. Michaels Terrace, in the hamlet a good thirty-minute walk. The moon was bright, so he had plenty of light and as he reached Silver Hill by the Homewood House estate at about 11.10pm he noticed a pair of feet sticking out onto the path.

Obviously curious William took a closer look and discovered a prostrate man on the ground with his head towards the hedge and he looked asleep. He spoke to the man, who had his eyes closed, and he mumbled back. William thought it was the taller one of the hawkers he had seen in the Eight Bells, Salem, but wasn't a hundred percent sure. Unable to rouse him he decided to leave him be as he knew what it was like when you'd had a few too many beers.

At about 11.30pm Frank Mitchell, a butcher who lived in Tenterden, was returning from Biddenden in his carriage along the Ashford road entering St Michaels when he passed three foreign looking men walking in the direction of the Church. He could not identify them in the moonlight as he was high up, but he noticed one was carrying something over his shoulder. The men stopped and watched him pass by.

At about the same time Sarah Appleyard was at her bedroom window in the school house overlooking the road and church. She was tired after her long day but as it was such a beautiful bright moonlit night she decided to take in the view of the church before closing the curtains. She was standing admiring the scene, when she spotted what she believed were the two hawkers heading up the hill one behind the other talking to each other. She couldn't believe the coincidence of seeing them yet again. She was the last one to see Iddir alive.

*

2:

Saturday Morning 17 June 1905

There had been several heavy downpours during the early hours, but by dawn it had cleared to a warm sunny morning and steam was rising from the wet ground. Abigail Eldridge lived in a rural cottage just outside Ewhurst, a mile from the picturesque village of Bodiam, and eight miles south west of Tenterden. She had risen early at 5.30am just as the sun was rising as was her custom because she enjoyed the long June mornings. She was standing in the doorway of her cottage breathing in the warm air when she spotted two foreign looking men approaching along the road heading towards Bodiam. One was young and short and the other older and taller. As they came level, they stopped and approached her garden gate. She did not feel threatened but was wary and kept a firm hold on the door ready to slam it if necessary.

She was fascinated by the young one's fez and the taller one's large moustache which was curled up at the ends. He spoke to her, 'Which way Bodiam, missus?'

Abigail replied, 'Just continue down the hill, you can't miss it.'

'How far please?'

'Not far.'

'Thank you, missus.' And with that they rushed off as "fast as they could down the hill."

But it appears they may have missed the turning and taken a side lane further on the right that took them all the way to the Junction road, or they may have reached Bodiam, famous for its moated castle, not known what to do in the middle of the night and vaguely headed in the direction of Robertsbridge. Either way Herbert Simmons, a Robertsbridge blacksmith, was sitting in the Junction Inn near the village of Sandhurst, between Bodiam and Robertsbridge when Salem and Ben Ali came in about 6.00am. The Inn was a large weatherboard seventeenth century coaching inn at what was then a major junction. At the time of writing the book it is a restaurant. Pub licensing in the period were extensive and drinks could be had from five or six in the morning until midnight. He knew Salem having seen him around Robertsbridge, so he spoke to him, 'What are you doing here this early my friend. You're wet through. What have you been up to?'

Salem said, 'Been in Wadhurst. Been out since two this morning.'

'Whose you're friend?' Herbert asked looking at the dishevelled and wet Ben Ali.

Salem did not reply, but Ben Ali did, 'Do you know when train to Tenterden?'

It appears that the two were under the impression that it was possible to catch a train near there. There was in fact a small halt called Junction Road with a platform made of earth and wood, but no station building.

'Sorry, lad, I have no idea,' replied Herbert who noticed he was holding two rugs under his coat. 'There is a halt here, but trains rarely stop. You'll have to go to Bodiam or Robertsbridge to get one, but they don't operate this early. Why not have a drink and rest up a bit?'

They stayed according Herbert until nearly seven drying out and having a drink before walking up the road towards Bodiam. Edwin Pullen, a local postman from Hawkhurst was freewheeling his bicycle down Bodiam hill and enjoying the breeze at about 6.30am and passed the same two foreigners heading towards Robertsbridge. He thought it strange being so early and far from a village and wondered where they had come from.

For reasons unclear after leaving the Junction Inn they decided to split up and Ben Ali headed back to Bodiam in search of a train and Salem continued on his quest to find Robertsbridge. At 7.45am Ada Roberts, the daughter of the landlord of the Castle Inn in Bodiam was busy cleaning the bar in readiness for the days customers when a damp and dishevelled Ben Ali entered the Inn and asked for a pint of ale. She poured him a glass and he sat down in a corner. She furtively watched him as she continued cleaning, and he seemed in an agitated state and was sweating. He enquired when the next train was due for Robertsbridge. The Inn overlooks the small railway station situated by the River Rother on the railway line between Tenterden and Robertsbridge. She checked the time and told him it was due any minute and he ran off to catch it leaving his glass half full. She watched him running down the road from the doorway but didn't see anyone else.

At 8am Edward, was in his usual position watching the world go by in the butcher shop doorway in Robertsbridge when he saw Salem coming along the road from the direction of Salehurst. He hailed him and Salem walked over to him. Edward asked, 'What have you been up to. You look as though you've been out all night: you're all wet through. You should go home and change before you catch something.'

'Me come from Wadhurst. Out all night.'

'Out all night, eh. Got a girlfriend have you?'

Salem didn't answer, but Edward could see he was quite distressed.

'How about a cup of tea. I was just about to make one for me self.'

Edward made him a cup of tea and they stood in the doorway drinking it, but Salem was very quiet.

*

At about 10am, 15-year-old Charlie Fox, left his house at 13 St Michaels Terrace, a row of agricultural labourers' cottages which were positioned along Grange Road. He lived there with his parents, Charles and Kate, his four sisters and two brothers and usually went on a Saturday errand to collect mushrooms for his mother.

He climbed over the back fence of his garden which led to orchards and fields known locally as Churchfields as they were adjacent to the village church. He had a basket with him and knew the best spots to find the mushrooms, so he headed off enjoying the warm June morning. It had rained during the night and the grass was damp. He walked up towards the church and into Churchfield and then headed towards the trees at the top bordering Shoreham Lane. It was a good spot for mushrooms. As he approached the area he saw a man lying in the grass. He was sleeping with one arm under his body and the other down his side. It looked as though he was wearing a red cap. Charlie thought it strange for someone to be sleeping there. He was concerned he might be a tramp, or a drunk recovering from a Friday night in the Crown Inn and he was too scared to venture close. He thought if he disturbed him he might get angry and so he walked to another area of the field. He didn't mention his encounter to his parents when he got home. The day passed like any other Saturday.

It was probably a wise decision by him not to have approached, as what he would have seen was the image of nightmares. The man wasn't sleeping but was dead with his throat cut, and what he thought was a red cap was in fact congealed blood where the man had been bludgeoned round the head.

*

On the morning of Sunday 18 the village had roused itself early and slowly and a sizeable congregation had listened intently to a sermon by Reverend John Jarvis, the vicar of St Michaels church. He was always pleased to welcome so many devotees and was satisfied they had enjoyed his sermon and had gone home happy. Little did he realise that by evening he would be counselling and consoling many of them. On leaving the church many of the villagers had dispensed with their Sunday best. The wives began preparing meals for their families and by early afternoon mothers were settling down to keep watch over their children and all was peaceful in the traditional English village where life seemed so far away from the problems of the world.

At about 2pm, two young friends, 20-year-old David Collins and 22-year-old James Blackman, both agricultural workers, decided to go for a walk to make the most of the fine weather. They set off from Collin's house situated behind the Crown Inn and walked up the lane towards the Churchfield. They went up through St. Michaels churchyard and walked through the orchard belonging to Mr Bugden which bordered the west side of the field, with Ashford Road on their right one and Shoreham Lane at the top. A housing development and Orchard Road now covers the whole area. They were both in good spirits and having a joke and chat. Collins was looking over the hedge at a small copse of trees when he noticed a swarm of flies hovering over the long grass which was awaiting cutting for hay. He could just make out a dark shape. He suddenly stopped and his companion nearly went into the back of him.

'Hey Jim, can you see that swarm of flies over there in the corner?'

'See 'em, I can hear them,' he replied.

'Must be a big animal carcass to attract that lot. We ought to check.'

'Do we have to,' said Jim without enthusiasm. 'Oh, all right go on then. It's probably only a dead village dog anyway.'

David Collins climbed over the fence and walked towards the swarm in the north-west corner of the field bordering Shoreham Lane. James Blackman followed behind and was suddenly startled by a loud exclamation from his friend who was a few yards ahead of him.

'Oh my God!'

'Whatever's wrong?' answered Blackman worried that something had happened to him.

'It's not a dog,' he exclaimed, 'It's a body of a man with his throat cut, it's awful.'

Blackman came up beside him. On seeing the prone body covered in blood and flies and with the putrid smell hitting him, he gasped and put his hand to his mouth before quickly averting his eyes. Neither of the young men had ever seen such a sight before and were not keen to get any closer. The man was obviously dead. Both men needed a few minutes to get over the shock. Being a hot June day and having laid there for so long the body had attracted a lot of flies and insects, but luckily no crows.

'I had better fetch the Bobbies. You wait over the fence there by the road,' Collins said to his mate.

David went sprinting down the lane heading for the Crown Inn to raise the alarm, just three hundred yards down the road while Blackman stood guard by the road.

*

Local Police Constable Albert James Byerley was having a surreptitious quiet Sunday afternoon doze behind the desk at Tenterden Police Station. The station was situated in the shadow of St Mildreds church in the centre of the high street about two miles from the scene of the murder. Sundays were always quiet once the noise of bells and churchgoers had subsided in the morning. Having a nap on duty was a serious breach of regulations and if caught he would be severely dealt with, but Saturday night had been busy dealing with the usual drunkenness and fights. Being a policeman was an exhausting vocation as they were on duty twenty-fours, three hundred and sixty-five days a year with no days off or holidays. His only recent respite had been when he fell over in the dark chasing a poacher resulting in a damaged ankle. But even then he had to hobble in to man the desk after a couple of days rest. Tenterden police only consisted of Sergeant Thomas Sales and three constables, one of which being Albert and he was relatively confident that the sarge would not catch him.

He was therefore somewhat startled and nearly fell off his chair when an out of breath and panicky David Collins came hurtling through the door screaming, 'there's been a murder!' He knew David as he did most people in the district and after adjusting his uniform he calmed the shaking young man and ascertained the facts.

'Now calm down David and tell me what all this fuss is about.'

'I've just told you. There's been a murder,' repeated a frustrated David.

'I heard that, but where and who has been murdered?'

'There's a man lying dead in the field beyond the church in St Michaels.'

'You're sure he's dead and not sleeping?'

'Of course I am! He stinks and there's blood everywhere and his throat is cut.'

'Do you recognise him?'

'No. He's not local and he is dressed funny.'

'His throat is cut you say; that does sound like murder.'

27-year-old Albert was a relatively old hand with seven years under his belt. He was London born and streetwise and had followed in the footsteps of his father who was still a police sergeant in London. But Albert's experience on the beat in a small country town had not put him in such a situation before. Bodies with their throats cut were not a common occurrence, particularly on a Sunday afternoon.

He locked the station and hailed a passing carter, commandeering a lift to St Michaels. The only form of transport the local police had at that time was by horseback, cab, train or on foot. They had no vehicles of their own not even a bicycle. In cases of emergency like this the police had to rely on the good will of anyone who owned a cart or carriage to help; either that or run all the way and Albert wasn't keen to do that on a hot June afternoon. There was no telephone system and so on the way he stopped off at a colleague's house and raised the alarm with him asking him to inform Sergeant Sales. Albert and David arrived on the scene at 3.15pm much to the relief of Blackman and he soon took control. The word had already gone out around the hamlet about the discovery and a small gathering of concerned villagers had collected to sneak a view of the grisly scene.

He approached the group and shouted, 'Now then you lot. Clear off! I can't have you trampling all over the place. This is serious. Go home all of you.'

'Come on Albert you can't blame us. Nothing like this has ever happened around here before.'

'Constable if you please. Now off with you,' he repeated but of course they all ignored him.

'Where's the body David' he asked Collins.

'Over there in the far corner just below the fir trees,' he replied. 'It's a horrible sight his throat has been cut wide open and his head smashed in.'

'OK, calm down. You stay here and don't leave. Nor you Jim Blackman. You'll have to be interviewed later and make a statement.'

He retrieved his notebook and pencil from his breast pocket and gingerly approached the body. He immediately recoiled at the sight and smell of the corpse as it was already putrefying, but saw that Collins wasn't exaggerating about the severity of the injuries. This was going to be a murder case and with no one else available it was up to him to make the first observations. Police constables had no real training particularly in regard to investigation and most just used their initiative and learned on the job. He realised senior officers would be arriving at some point to take over and would want a detailed report. It was not a pretty sight, but he steeled himself and knew he couldn't afford to be squeamish.

The body was cold and stiff and was lying almost on its back and the throat was indeed cut wide open with the windpipe cut through. He noted that the body was lying diagonally with the head towards Shoreham Lane, a lane that ran along the top of the field and the feet towards the small copse in the corner. He knelt down swiping the flies away and could see the back of the skull was caved in and a bone was protruding and was lying flat on the bloodied hair. He examined the dead man's hands but there was no blood on them. He noticed a cut on the left side of the neck and the pocket and shirt were stained with blood. Blood had also seeped from the right groin. He couldn't see a hat anywhere.

The clothes were not disarranged in any way but were shabby. He was wearing a blue serge jacket and trousers, a black and grey check cloth waistcoat, blue and white checked shirt, odd worsted socks, one blue and one grey, and old blucher boots mended at the toe end with wire to keep the sole on. These were a popular old-style boot at the time with side pieces over the front and open laces making them easy to lace and more comfortable to wear, similar to a modern work boot. The trousers and waistcoat were buttoned up and he had a bright red sash round his waist. Albert immediately deduced that the dead man must be foreign. He didn't think that anyone round here would be wearing such an item. The thought made him smile and relieved his anxiety somewhat. He put all these details in his notebook. Having made detailed notes of the body and surrounds he then proceeded to search the body and found a silver 4-shilling piece, a piece of rag in the left-hand pocket and a small knife in the waistcoat watch pocket. He stood up pleased with himself. He fancied he might make a detective one day. He went back to the road and was pleased to see one of his colleagues from the town arriving at a pace.

'I can't believe it. A murder here, I can't believe it,' he repeated.

'Well believe it, the body is just a few yards over there. Nasty business.'

'The sergeant will be here soon, and he has sent a message to Superintendent Thomas Fowle.'

The Kent County Constabulary was divided into twelve divisions each with a superintendent in charge. Thomas Fowle was in charge of the local division based in the town of Cranbrook some eight miles west of Tenterden.

'I'll take a look.' Continued Albert's colleague.

'No lad, better stay here. Don't want the scene disturbed,' he said professionally. 'Now you lot get back will you,' he shouted at the crowd again.

'Bet you a shilling lad that the superintendent gets his son onto this,' stated Albert.

'Who's his son?' asked the other.

'Detective Sergeant Fowle of course.'

'What from that Maidstone lot. Why call him?'

'Well for a start e's the best damned detective we've got that's why, and they have to deal with the really bad cases like this. He's like a ferret down a rabbit hole when it comes to chasing out villains. Never gives up until he tracks them down.'

'I've never met him but have heard of him. I believe he's known as the "terrier" by some of the real villains. Wasn't he involved in that famous Tonbridge murder case?'

'Sure was, back in 1901. New Year's Eve in fact. Tragic affair it was. A seven-year-old girl was murdered and dumped in a pond. He got the fella who did it and was commended for it. If he catches the bugger who did this he'll make Inspector for sure.'

They then stood guard awaiting the arrival of help.

*

Churchfield
Body found top of
this field under tree

St Michaels church and school showing Churchfield in the background. The orchard and copse were situated in the far-left corner behind the church. The inquest was held in the school. The house just visible behind the school is from where Sarah Appleyard last saw Iddir from her bedroom window. In the foreground are the allotments from where William Roberts watched the two hawkers pass by. [Postcard image/author collection]

St Michaels hamlet. The Crown Pub (left centre) where Iddir spent his last evening doing a roaring trade selling out his stock before heading back towards Tenterden and meeting up with Ben Ali. [Tenterden archive]

Silver Hill between Tenterden and St Michaels. The Fat Ox (on right) is where George Bassett met Iddir and Ben Ali on his way home at 11.15pm looking for accommodation an hour before Iddir was murdered. [Tenterden archive]

David Collins and James Blackman who found the body attend the Coroner's inquest. [Daily Mirror, 20th. June 1905]

3:

Detective Edwin Fowle Summoned

Constable Byerley was about to win his bet, for while they were speaking District Superintendent Thomas Fowle, was in the process of contacting his son, Detective Sergeant Edwin Fowle, by telegram and asking for his assistance as was the Constabulary policy since the detective department was created. The murder had taken place within his divisional area, and it was the responsibility of the detectives to investigate and liaise with him. The superintendent lived above the police station in an apartment and was a veteran officer of 43 years, having joined the police in 1862. He was due to serve another ten years before retiring in 1915 and become one of the longest serving officers in the force with 53 years under his belt. Thomas made arrangements to travel to Tenterden to be briefed.

He knew immediately that the case would need the expertise of his son, who had already investigated many high profile murder cases in his short career and was a highly experienced and respected officer and admired by his colleagues.

35-year-old First-Class Detective Sergeant Edwin Fowle was not a tall man at five feet nine inches tall but was broad shouldered, of stout stature and maintained a large moustache below a substantial nose. Being a plain clothes officer he was always well turned out wearing a fashionable derby hat. He took great care to dress smartly as he reckoned it gave him an air of authority and he liked to set a standard for his men. Although regulations insisted his jacket should have pockets that could accommodate a truncheon and handcuffs he ignored the need for a truncheon. He was a religious man, had a somewhat questioning mind and a tenacious nature, perfect attributes for a detective. He never knew what the day would bring, but it was the uncertainty which excited him.

He had joined the Kent police force ten years earlier on October 10, 1890, and moved into the dormitory barracks at their headquarters at Wrens Court in Maidstone for training before serving in several towns around the County of Kent over the next six years. He came from a police family and followed in his father's footsteps as had his elder brother Thomas also a sergeant and one of his uncles was in the police before becoming a railway detective. He was immediately acknowledged as a rising star and when the detective branch was formed in 1896 he was immediately selected to join them as a detective constable. He was in fact one of the first three detective constables on the force; a founding member of the department. Four years later in 1900, his diligence, intelligence and obvious aptitude for the work made him the clear choice to replace his boss Detective Sergeant George Foreman when he left. Edwin was promoted to First Class Detective Sergeant and assumed charge.

His appointment brought him back full circle to Maidstone and being single he faced the prospect of having to reside in the austere barrack living quarters with forty other single constables which he did not fancy. So he had immediately sought lodgings. He put the word out and luckily, a sergeant friend named John Kent heard of his plight and suggested inquiring with his elderly next door neighbour at 31 Melville Road, 74-year-old widowed Annie Smith, who sometimes took in lodgers. She didn't hesitate in welcoming him as having a policeman in the house made her feel really secure, not that he spent much time there being always on call and often leaving at all hours. What had initially been somewhat disconcerting for him was that Annie had two spinster daughters Maria and Margaret living with her, who although ten years older than him gave him a lot of attention. But he did get mothered and looked after well and it was cheap. It was an ongoing joke from the ladies in the house that he wasn't getting any younger and should be finding himself a wife, an idea that Edwin didn't object to, but finding the time for such endeavours was difficult with his erratic lifestyle. He had been lodging there for nearly five years and he found them convenient being only a few hundred yards from the headquarters, enabling him to walk to work.

He was having a rare spell of relaxation reviewing some paperwork while sitting in the back garden of his lodgings unaware that he was about to be plunged into yet another high-profile murder case.

Maria appeared at the back door, 'You have a visitor,' she informed him.

Standing behind her was the familiar figure of Tom Luck. Tom was 31-year-old Detective Constable Thomas James Luck. Whereas his sergeant was always immaculately dressed, he went for the more casual look with a straw boater hat perched on top of his head, a large moustache and often creased clothes.

'Urgent one for you sergeant, just in,' said Tom formally, 'and a bad one if you don't mind me saying.' He thrust a telegram into his hand.

Edwin read the telegram and his face soon turned to a grimace.

'Yes Tom, it appears so. It does sound like a bad one. You'll of course be my right-hand man.'

'Thanks, sarge. I guessed so. I've already got a cab waiting outside.'

'Glad to hear it.'

They had known each other for a while and had worked on many cases together forging a good working relationship and could recognise each other's moods. As they passed the parlour Edwin poked his head round the door and spoke to Maria.

'I'm off and I doubt whether I shall be back for dinner,' he apologised.

'Nothing unusual about that,' she laughed and went back to her embroidery.

As they left the house Edwin asked Tom, 'What do we know?'

'Only sketchy information at the moment, but a body has been found in a field in the hamlet of St Michaels at Tenterden. Pretty badly mutilated by all accounts.'

The two detectives climbed into the waiting carriage which set off at a pace with the two men being thrown about. It traversed the rough roads through the villages of Sutton Valence, Headcorn, and Biddenden finally reaching the hamlet of St Michaels an hour later. The carriage pulled up at a gate just before reaching the church where there was a throng of villagers surrounding two constables.

Constable Byerley gave an audible sigh of relief and welcomed the arrivals as they stepped out of the black carriage to be met by a clamour of voices. He saluted and gave his detailed report to Edwin, explaining the sequence of events leading up to his arrival. Some of the crowd recognised him and there were murmurs of 'It must be serious, that's Detective Sergeant Fowle.'

'Well done Constable Byerley. A good report. Can you show us to the body please.'

'I'm afraid there's no gate at the end of the field where the body is so we'll have to walk across to it,' apologised Byerley.

'No matter,' said Edwin and followed the constable.

The two detectives took in the scene, searched the vicinity, and noticed blood stains in the grass about two feet from the head. There was a slight depression in the grass as if the head had laid there at some point. Byerley showed them the items taken off the body.

'Well, obviously the man is foreign what with the scarlet sash and all,' commented Tom.

'Definitely. I would say Albanian or Turkish perhaps.'

'What on earth was he doing down here?' queried Tom.

'He's a hawker and was selling round here all-day Friday by all accounts,' interjected Byerley.

'Well, business cannot have been good if this is all the money he had on him,' replied Edwin holding the silver four-shilling piece in his hand.

Tom said, 'Perhaps he did though, and this is the result of a robbery gone wrong.'

'Maybe. But I cannot see any obvious sign of a struggle.'

'Looks as though he was hit from behind.'

'But why in the middle of a field. An attack would normally be on the road or somewhere secluded?' questioned Edwin.

'Yes it is strange.'

'And why cut his throat?'

'Perhaps the assailant panicked,' suggested Tom.

Having examined the body Edwin searched further afield but could not see any tracks but about twenty yards from where the body was lying, there was an area of flattened grass, as if someone else had been lying there as well. About four feet away and two feet from the bloodstain he found a stout cherry wood stick locally known as a "bat."

'Look what I've found,' he shouted over to Tom.

Tom walked towards him and looked down into the long grass where Edwin was pointing.

'The murder weapon!,' exclaimed Tom.'

Edwin crouched down to inspect it closely and could see hair and blood embedded at the end of it. It looked freshly cut. 'Well it's got blood and hair on it so it has something to do with it.'

'Knocked out with it then finished off with a knife,' said Tom gruesomely.

'You could be right. So, we have no idea who this is, where he came from, why he was attacked or when it happened,' declared Edwin.

'I still go for the robbery gone wrong,' repeated Tom.

'We need to start finding answers to some of these questions. First thing is to get a doctor to examine the body, so that we can get an idea of when death occurred. And get someone to organise accommodation for us. It'll be too late to travel home as this is looking like an all-nighter.'

'I'll get it organised,' said Tom

'By the state of the body I'd say he's been here a while,' observed Edwin.

'I agree, but if it has been, I am amazed nobody noticed it until now.'

'There's no footpath through here and the grass has been left to grow for hay so no reason to come in here,' Byerley informed them.

'We need to get on top of this quickly, Tom. I understand from Byerley here that there has been an outcry already by some of the locals and you know where that can lead. At least we have the light for a few more hours so let's get the local constables to start house to house inquiries. Start with this lot here,' he said indicating the assembled onlookers. 'Get them to stop anyone they encounter on the street and canvas the pub. We need witnesses and suspects. Let's get started then. Can we get the body moved somewhere private?'

'Arrangements have been made to place it in the stable at the Crown Inn.' Byerly informed them. It was common practice for public houses or the barns of nearby farms to be used to temporarily hold bodies in these circumstances until such time a post mortem had been arranged.

Two constables then gingerly covered the body and used a borrowed handcart to move it to the Crown conveniently located just a couple of hundred yards down the road from where the murder took place.

*

Bill Reeves was the 44-year-old landlord of the Crown Inn situated on the main road in the centre of the village. He lived above it with his wife Phoebe and their two young children. The pub had been in his family for several decades with his father running it before him, but he couldn't remember a murder in the village and had never catered for a mutilated corpse on the premises. When the police came calling late on Sunday afternoon asking to store it, he wasn't too keen on having it plus a lot of police hanging around as it might put off his customers. But he needn't have worried as it had the opposite effect as the villagers were keen to be there to see first-hand what was happening. His wife Phoebe made sure their young kids were kept indoors and as far away from the stable as possible.

When the corpse was brought in by the policemen he was shocked by the state of it and even more shocked to see it was the hawker who had caused such a stir in his pub on Friday evening. He felt as though he had a connection to the person even though he had only been with him for a brief time. The detectives arrived soon after to take a closer look at the deceased. It was all very unsettling.

'Very understanding of you Mr Reeves to allow us to have the body here.' said Edwin as he entered the tavern.

'Least I could do under the circumstances,' lied Bill.

'We will try not to disturb you too much and be out of here as quickly as possible.'

'Would you gentleman like a drink by any chance?'

Tom looked expectant but Edwin responded, 'Perhaps later thank you all the same,' much to Tom's disappointment.

'Would you mind taking a look at the deceased to see if you recognise him as we are struggling to discover who he is. You may have seen him around at some stage.'

'I don't need a close look as I already know who it is,' exclaimed Bill, 'He came into the pub at about 8.30pm on Friday night selling his mats and tablecloths. Caused quite a stir and got on well with the customers. He's from a band of foreign hawkers. Four or five of them I'm told. They were in town all day. Didn't speak much English. Nice fella he was.'

'Do you know his name?'

'I don't rightly know, but he did a brisk trade and sold out his stock taking about two pounds in silver. I remember Mr Milton the baker bought the last set of table cloths off him, and they had a laugh about it. He offered the man a drink, but he wouldn't take one. I think he was an abstainer, but he stood drinks for all those who bought something off him.'

'Did he seem alright when he left?'

'He was in a right cheerful mood having sold everything.'

'What time did he leave?'

'Can't say exactly as there was a lot going on, but I reckon soon after ten.'

'Thank you Mr Reeves you have been immensely helpful.'

Edwin turned to Tom 'Well we now know he was alive late Friday evening. That's something.'

At that point Sergeant Thomas Sales, in charge of the Tenterden Police joined them.

'How is the search for witnesses going on?' he asked him.

'I think the men are getting a good response,' the sergeant replied.' 'It's hardly surprising considering the way they were dressed.'

'They were far from inconspicuous so loads of residents must have noticed them,' interjected Tom.

'I agree. Lucky for us I suppose in an investigation like this. Our first priority is to track down the rest of the band and quickly. Hopefully, they are staying in town somewhere.'

'Or absconded more likely,' stated Tom.

'We have found a possible valuable witness. I think you should come and speak to her,' the sergeant finally got a word in.

'Who is it?'

'It's a Mrs Appleyard the wife of the local school teacher. They live in the school house which has a view over the road and field, and she saw them last night.'

'Well, I'll be damned, this sound promising,' cried Edwin, 'We could have this case sown up in no time.'

'That'll be the day,' moaned Tom.

They left the pub and quickly walked to the school house about three hundred yards away and were shown into the lounge by John Appleyard the schoolmaster.

'Good evening Mrs Appleyard.'

'Good evening Inspector. Please call me Sarah.'

'I'm afraid I'm just a detective sergeant at the moment,' he responded embarrassed.

Out the corner of his eye he spotted Tom smirk. He was smiling because he guessed that if his boss cracked this case no doubt he would get a promotion to an Inspector.

'What a terrible occurrence. I cannot believe such a thing could happen in such a peaceful little village like this,' said Sarah Appleyard.

'Indeed, it is. Could you talk us through what you saw on Friday?'

'Well, quite a lot actually. Everywhere I went that day I bumped into them. I first saw these two strangely dressed gentleman at about 4pm. They were wearing red fez's you see so I thought they were Turkish. Not the usual kind you see. I was in the garden, and they walked past going towards Tenterden.'

'Could you describe them?' Edwin interrupted.

'Well, one was only young, noticeably shorter and slimmer than the other and he had black curly hair and a moustache.'

'And the other?' encouraged Edwin.

'Well, he was taller and older; and he also had a thin moustache.'

'He sounds like our victim.'

'I'm afraid so. And you say you saw them again?'

'I did. In the evening about 7.30pm when I was on my way into town they were sitting on the bench at Beacon Hill corner with their bundles beside them. Table cloths I think.'

'The same two?'

'Yes.'

'Were they acting normally?

'They were just resting by the look of it.'

'Was that the last time?'

'No. I was returning home from the town at about 10.40pm passed the younger man on his own walking towards the town.'

'No sign of the older one?'

'No.'

'Well as you said, you certainly kept coming across them.'

'But there's more sergeant. Just by coincidence I was looking out of my bedroom window just before midnight. It was a beautiful moonlit night and I saw two men walking up the hill out of the village wearing the distinctive hats. One was carrying a bundle over his shoulder. The other didn't appear to have anything. I watched them in the bright moonlight go up the road and then they climbed the bank by the roadside for a while and then went back onto the road by the Vicarage gate. I think they must have either turned into the meadow gate or went up the road known as Shoreham Lane just past the field where I lost sight of them. One was walking in front of the other and they appeared to be muttering to each other.'

'Were they arguing?'

'No, I think just whispering.'

'Do you think they were the same two men from earlier.'

'I only saw their backs, but I believe so.'

'In that case you may be the last person to see the victim alive.'

'Oh dear, really!' she exclaimed putting her hand to her mouth.

'Thank you Mrs Appleyard you have been unbelievably helpful. We will need a statement from you if that's all right while its fresh in your mind.'

When they left Edwin said to Tom, 'If they were the same two from earlier it looks as though the victim was alive at midnight. We are already starting to narrow it down.'

They walked back to the pub and found Sergeant Sales talking to Superintendent Thomas Fowle, dressed in his uniform with peaked cap who had just arrived from Cranbrook. It wasn't often that the two them worked on a case together and when it did occur it was a surreal situation. The superintendent greeted his son warmly. Thomas Fowle joined the Kent police in 1862 and eventually served for 53 years retiring in 1915. He had formed a celebrated police dynasty with three of his four sons also joining the Kent force. Edwin's older brother Thomas joined in 1890 and his younger brother Ivo in 1900 both retiring in 1930. Between them they had an aggregate family service of an incredible 265 years.

'I understand you have already found a promising witness,' he asked.

'I believe so. Have you had a chance to see the body yet?' he asked his father.

'I have. A particularly brutal and vicious assault. Whoever did it must had some massive grudge against him.'

'So you don't think the motive was robbery?' he asked his father while winking at Tom.

'Some kind of revenge or hate driven attack I would say,' confirmed his father.

He trusted his father's opinion who with his decades of experience and dealings with many murders under his belt knew what he was talking about.

'That's my initial feelings too.'

'Beating someone senseless and almost slicing their head off seems over the top for a robbery.'

'Do we know how many men were in this gang?'

'I've heard recently from various villages locally that there are several in the group working the area, but not sure exactly how many,' Sergeant Sales informed them.

'What's your next move Edwin?'

'We are already canvassing the area for witnesses and obviously someone might be able to tell us where these guys are.'

'Let's hope so as we may an extremely dangerous man loose in the area capable of who knows what. I'll obviously give you all the help I can, and telegrams and messages had been sent out to all police stations across Kent and particularly the local ports like Folkestone. All the village bobbies in the area will be given a description and asked if they know of this band of hawkers and particularly this young man. Fingers crossed we'll hear news soon.'

*

Artist impression of a young Ferat Ben Ali with "boyish looks," arrested at the Star Inn, Ashford on Monday morning by Constable Apps. [The People, Sunday 25 June 1905/British Newspaper Archive.]

Artists sketch of Handj ou Iddir who made such an impression on the customers in the Crown Inn on Friday evening. [The People Sunday 25 June 1905/British Newspaper Archive]

4:

Arrests and the Investigation Begins

28-year-old Constable Thomas Henry Cloke was based in Sandhurst, a quiet village right on the border with East Sussex where he lived a relatively peaceful life with little excitement being a rural beat. Some seven miles to the south west across the border was the town of Robertsbridge which was out of his jurisdiction, but he had a close relationship with his colleagues in the Sussex force and often came in contact with them. Being so close to the town he would receive snippets of news and gossip from that area. When he heard of the manhunt for a young foreign hawker wanted in connection for a murder he was rather excited particularly as recently he had heard about two foreigners of that description lodging in Robertsbridge at a local inn. He immediately sent a message to Edwin of this possible sighting and received word back to try and liaise with the East Sussex force to detain them and take them to Cranbrook police station.

At midnight on Sunday in Robertsbridge, situated fourteen miles to the west of Tenterden, Constable Cloke was standing outside the Railway Tavern where the suspects were allegedly staying with two colleagues from the Sussex force. The pub had originally been built to house Irish navvies who were constructing the main railway line from London, and it had always had a reputation for drunkenness and bad behaviour. It was closed in the 1920s. Cloke and the others were well aware of this when they arrived and decided to proceed with caution.

'Remember lads, these men have been reported to be armed with knives and don't speak much English so be careful. We don't want anyone hurt and we need to get 'em quick, surprise them.'

He banged on the door of the pub. He had seen lights on and knew someone was up and about. The door was answered by the landlord, and he explained what they were there to do. The landlord directed them to a room at the back but wasn't happy about the late-night intrusion. The three officers walked stealthily with their lamps to the room where Cloke knocked loudly.

Initially there was no response or sound of movement from inside. Then someone shouted, 'who there?'

'Police. Open up we need to speak to you.'

There was still no sound of movement.

'What do you think they are up to?' asked one of the constables.

'I don't know, but we need to get in there sharpish,' replied Cloke.

After a couple minutes or so, Cloke tried the handle and found it locked. 'Right let's not muck about lads kick it down,' he said to his colleagues and the door soon swung open. Holding up their lamps in the dark they found two men lying on their beds squinting up at them.

'Stay where you are and keep you or hands where we can see them. What are your names?' asked Cloke.

The two men tried to give their names but because of their pidgin English, their accents and their obvious fright the officers had great difficulty understanding and even more trouble trying to spell them. After several attempts they finally established their names as Frank Salem and Meznow Mohamed,

Constable Cloke asked Salem, 'Where were you on Friday night?'

Frank Salem looked at the constable rather mystified as if trying to remember and finally answered 'Me business at Wadhurst,' which was a village some ten miles north west of Robertsbridge, a good three and a half mile walk away.

'Are you sure of that?'

'Yes sir.'

'And you?' he asked Meznow.

'Me at business Netherfield.'

'Are you sure you weren't in the town of Tenterden Friday night?'

'Me at business at Wadhurst Friday night,' repeated Salem, 'Me don't know Tenterden.'

The constable then cautioned them. In 1905 there was no official requirement or law for a constable to say anything to a suspect, but they were advised to "Keep your eyes and your ears open, and your mouth shut." However, although there was no official national caution, they were encouraged to say to an accused person "that you are not bound to say anything tending to criminate yourself, and that anything you say may be used against you," before making a statement or just to read out their warrant and tell the person why they were being arrested.

'Well either way you are both under arrest on suspicion of being concerned in a murder.'

He cautioned them and told them they were being taken to a police station for questioning, and that they must be searched first. Speaking little English the caution did not really register with them and they both appeared petrified. They got up and dressed and Salem bent down and retrieved something from under the bed which he attempted to put in his scarlet waist sash.

'Ere, what you got there, hand it over now?' shouted Cloke.

'Me get money.'

Cloke retrieved a small bag from him and quickly examined it. It was heavy with gold and silver coins. In 1905 money was still minted from solid gold and solid silver. Gold coins included a Sovereign, a half Sovereign and the ten-shilling coin. The four shilling or Double Florin and five-shilling coin were made of silver.

'This seems a lot of money to have,' he said, 'Where did you get it?

'Me sell,' answered Salem.

'Business must be good,' he said holding the small bag up to the light of his lamp and shaking it.

The constables searched Salem and found a razor, clasp knife, tobacco pouch, pocket book, cigarette holder, a Kent and East Sussex railway timetable and some cheap jewellery. Mezrow only had six and a half pence in coppers. When the money found on Salem was counted it was discovered it amounted to thirty-four pounds and ten shillings in gold and one pound and eight shillings in silver.

The two suspects were transported to Cranbrook police station where Superintendent Fowle was there to greet them. He cautioned them again and quickly interviewed them to establish their names, ages, the relationship between them and their nationality. He also took charge of the money and personal items and clothing taken off the prisoners. No bloodstains were found on them. Up until that point the police had believed they were Albanians or similar but could now confirm they were Algerian. When informed of the death of Iddir they professed "great grief and surprise" particularly Salem the brother who was distraught. With the realisation that they might be in big trouble they both immediately claimed protection of the French consul. They were put in a cell for the rest of the night.

Edwin received news by messenger of the successful arrest and the prisoners' details. He now knew who the deceased was and a good idea of when he died plus he had two suspects in custody and all within twelve hours of finding the body. Not bad going he thought, but until he had interviewed them he wouldn't know if they were connected with the murder or involved.

*

In Ashford, a large market town 11 miles north of Tenterden, 22-year-old Constable Mark Apps was on the Sunday night duty and walking his beat along the quiet and deserted streets. It was the early hours of Monday morning and he was tired, more so as it had been a dreary and tedious shift with nothing exciting to report, not even the late-night drunks to deal with. He was looking forward to getting back to the station when the Royal Mail overnight trap came towards him. The driver pulled the horse up and he hailed Apps who could see that he appeared very excited about something.

'Anything wrong?' he asked.

'Have you heard?' asked the driver.

'Heard what?' asked Apps.

'There's been a terrible murder over in Tenterden.'

'Really.'

Yeh. Bloke got his head almost cut off, there saying.'

'Are you sure. Who's saying?'

'It's common knowledge over there. There's a man hunt for some foreign Arabs of some sort.'

'You don't say.'

The trap trotted off and Apps was now also excited as he had come across a couple of strangely dressed foreigners in the town the day before. They could have something to do with it. He knew they were staying at the Star Inn lodging house on East Hill in the town centre. He immediately rushed back to the station where the night officer was surprised that Apps knew about the murder as he had only just received a message about it himself. They agreed that they should detain them as soon as possible just in case. At 7am they were entering the rather rough looking Star Inn. The landlord, George Skinner was surprised by their early morning visit and when told the reason he informed them that the two men were there and directed Apps to their room. He knocked on the door and not getting an answer he shouted.

'It's the police. Open the door we need to speak to you on an urgent matter. Don't be afraid. We know you are in there.'

There was no answer, and no one came to the door.

'Alright then we will have to force entry. Stand back.'

The door proved to be unlocked, but they burst in anyway, to find two dejected and frightened teenage men standing in the corner. Like his colleagues in Robertsbridge, Apps had difficulty establishing their names but discovered they were Ferat Ben Ali and Daka Belkacem and established they were part of the same travelling group. He informed them of the death of Iddir and they were visibly shocked. They both

46

stood mumbling and Apps did not understand most of what they said. Ben Ali was shaking almost uncontrollably.

Apps asked Ben Ali, 'Where were you Friday evening?'

'I was in Robertsbridge.'

'Not in Tenterden?'

'No.'

'What about you?' he asked Belkacem.

Belkacem just stood staring at Apps and didn't answer as though in shock. He then searched the two of them and found eight pounds and ten shillings in gold in a little bag on Ben Ali and also found a watch, a penknife and a blood-stained handkerchief. Belkacem only had sixpence on him in his red waist sash.

He then cautioned them. The prisoners did not offer any resistance and were escorted first to Ashford police station. The news of the arrest was conveyed to Edwin in Tenterden who was really delighted at the actions of the two constables in detaining the men so quickly. He told Tom Luck to get over to Ashford and transport them back to Tenterden police station. During the carriage ride Belkacem slouched dejectedly but Ben Ali took a great interest in the passing countryside to the surprise of Tom. He did not seem in anyway concerned and as they reached St Michaels he turned to Tom and said: 'Where are we?'

'I would think you'd recognise it,' replied Tom sardonically.

'Me don't know.'

'We are passing through the village of St. Michaels.' Tom informed him watching his reaction.

'Oh, me never been here before, anytime.'

*

The Tenterden Town Police station was housed in a small corner building in the centre of the High Street backing on to the scenic St. Mildred's Church and its churchyard. It was in the narrowest part of the street and had once functioned as a toll house with a barrier across the road. It had a clear view down the western half of the High Street from the front door. A constable often stood outside and watched the world go by. It also served as the town's lock up for the temporary holding of prisoners until they were released or moved on to prison. On the upper floor there was a small Victorian style wood panelled courtroom used for magistrate and Coroner hearings. The prisoners had all been placed in one cell which was a regulation procedure and had been kept under constant guard to ensure there was no argument or trouble between them as Salem and Ben Ali did not appear to be on friendly terms.

Superintendent Fowle arrived to be present when they were interviewed. They were introduced to the four prisoners by Tom. Edwin was rather taken aback at how young and dejected the three youngsters were. Not the band of cutthroats he for some reason had imagined. Frank Salem was a different persona altogether. Swarthy, tall and stout he was far more menacing in looks. He continued to profess that he had never visited Tenterden.

He actually felt sorry for them. Ben Ali was short and looked as though a puff of wind would blow him over. He reckoned he couldn't weigh more than eight or nine stone. He was a good-looking lad with a pencil moustache and black curly hair. Belkacem and Meznow looked even younger and were similar in height and weight. They had already been cautioned, searched and given new outer clothing. Edwin had laid out all of Ben Ali's belongings on a table which included a handkerchief which had possible blood stains on it and a shirt and jersey with traces of blood on the inside of the collar. He asked Ben Ali to confirm they were his which he did.

'Can you account for the blood on the handkerchief and your clothes?' he asked him, indicating the stains with hand signals to make it clear what he was asking.

He replied, 'Me have nose bleed.'

Later Edwin did the same with Salem and he confirmed that a knife, razor and clothing was his.

None of them were willing to make a statement and communication without an interpreter was difficult so they were not pressurised to do so but were left to be interviewed later. After seeing the prisoners Edwin handed the superintendent thirty-five pounds eighteen shillings and six pence found on Salem and the eight pound and ten shillings on Ben Ali. Edwin asked the station sergeant to send all these exhibits to Dr Joyce, a local surgeon proficient at forensic examination for analysis including a sample of Iddir's hair in a bottle received from Doctor Matthews.

Later he was sitting at a desk in the rear office when a constable came in to announce that Mr Murton was there to see him about organising the inquest. Mr Charles D Murton was the District Coroner for the Cranbrook district which covered St Michaels. He lived in a large house named Cranbrook Hall in the town, which was 8 miles to the west of Tenterden. He was a familiar figure in the area and was known as the "Major" due to his honorary rank bestowed on him for being commander of the Cranbrook Company of the territorial battalion of the Buffs, a County regiment. He was also senior partner of the law firm Murton, Clarke and Murton-Neale and a Clerk to the Justices. He was a stocky 39-year-old with the obligatory moustache of the time and was always well attired and like Edwin wore a derby hat.

'Good morning Major.'

'Good morning Edwin, how are you?'

'Fine thanks.'

'I understand you have made two arrests?'

'Better than that we have now made four. Another two in Ashford earlier this morning.' Edwin said triumphantly.

'Really!,' exclaimed the Major. 'Good show.'

'A constable over there recognised their description immediately.'

'The benefit of having local bobbies on the beat. That's really good news. Any indication whether any of them are the culprits?'

'Far too early to say, I'm afraid.'

'I spoke to your father on the way over who has promised to keep me informed of developments.'

'That's good.'

The Major knew the family very well particularly his father as he lived in the same village and because of his position as Coroner whereby he often had dealings with the superintendent.

'As you are aware the inquest has to be heard within forty-eight hours of the deceased dying so we are up against it, but I have formed a jury, and we are holding a preliminary hearing tonight at St Michael's school. Of course, you will be required to be there. It won't take long as it's just a formality and I will adjourn it to give you time for your investigation,' continued the Major.

'Not a problem. I will see you there. I am off to the Crown Inn to meet with the doctor who is hopefully going to tell us the cause of death, so if you'll excuse me.'

As they were leaving the police station a flustered Charles Fox, father of Charlie Fox junior came in to see Edwin to inform him of his son's encounter on Saturday morning. He was very apologetic but said that it was only when his son heard him telling his wife Kate about the finding of the body that his son told them. Edwin asked him to bring Charlie to the station so he could give a statement and warned the father that he might be required to attend the inquest at some stage and possibly the trial.

'Now we're starting to get somewhere,' he muttered to himself.

*

Dr Matthews, a practicing doctor in Tenterden arrived at the Crown stable at 9am on Monday morning to examine the body while the two detectives looked on. He checked the man's clothing and pockets and closely examined the neck, head, hands and feet and then stood back and contemplated for a couple of minutes.

Edwin ever impatient asked, 'Any idea when the deceased died Doctor. We really need to know urgently?'

'From what I can tell I should say sometime on Friday night or early Saturday. It will need a post mortem for me to be more detailed.

'And cause of death?' he persisted.

'Well, I can see most of the injuries and my initial reaction is that it looks a bit complicated. He has got this deep wound across his throat which looks as though it was caused by several cuts. It's a hell of a cut, about seven inches long. Nearly taken his head off. I'd say it was viciously done as the cuts are ragged. There are two superficial wounds on his throat and two others on the left angle of jaw. See here,' he said pointing for them to take a look.

They leaned forward but not too closely preferring to take the doctor's word for it.

'I see. What kind of knife did the deed do you think?'

'Probably a long sharp one but could have been a shorter one by the way someone has hacked at his throat. Whoever did it was in a hurry and really wanted to make sure he was dead.'

'And the head wounds?'

'Obviously done by that hefty stick left by the body that you showed me. Doesn't take a genius to work that out. Again I'll need to examine it more closely at the P.M. but there appears to be several fractures of the skull and as you can see plenty of blood as the hair is matted with it.'

'Preliminary cause of death then, Doctor?'

'I would say he was bludgeoned with considerable force first possible more than once and because of the lack of blood from his throat, the poor man was alive when struck, and his throat was cut later. Oh, and the deceased's left ear escaped injury which indicates he was probably lying on his side and was struck from above and behind.

I noticed that there are blood stains outside and inside the trouser pockets caused by someone putting their bloodstained hands inside.'

'Told you he was robbed,' interjected Tom.

'Thank you doctor that has answered a lot.'

After the doctor had left, Edwin asked Belkacem if he could face formally identifying his Uncle's body as he wasn't sure Salem could cope or would cause a scene. Belkacem agreed and was escorted to the stable for the gruesome and upsetting task. Having seen the body he confirmed that it was Hadj ou Iddir and the leader of their group. It was obviously an extremely upsetting experience for the lad.

*

The Railway Tavern, Robertsbridge on the left where P.C Cloke arrested Frank Salem and "Oily" just after midnight on Monday morning after kicking down the bedroom door. [Postcard image/John Brookland]

The Star Inn, East Hill, Ashford where Ben Ali and Belkacem were arrested early Monday morning by Constable Apps. [pubwiki.co.uk]

5:

A Flurry of Activity

'Tom we are going on a train ride to Robertsbridge.'

'What now. For what?'

'Three reasons Tom. I like trains and I want to see this new Kent & East Sussex train line they have built here and secondly we need to interview some of their employees to establish the movements of our suspects. They seem to have spent a lot of their time on the new railway so someone down there must have seen them.'

'And the third reason?' queried Tom.

'It will be a darn sight more comfortable than by horse and carriage.'

They walked out of the front door of the police station and headed straight down the High Street, with the town's famous avenue of trees and green lawns stretching out in front of them.

'Beautiful town this,' commented Edwin as he looked down the street. 'So wide and open and looking colourful in this lovely warm June sunshine.'

'Postcard pretty and so busy,' agreed Tom watching all the carts and carriages trotting by and dodging the many shoppers in their finery.

'Well, it's the main shopping centre for miles around and I believe it is growing in size very quickly. The railway will bring more visitors and prosperity no doubt,' commented Edwin.

'I understand they have a good livestock market here with hundreds of sheep driven down the street. Must be quite a sight,' said Tom.

After two hundred yards they reached a pub called the Vine Inn which had a well-known local brewery attached to it. Between it and a small quaint fire station there was a track leading down to the new Tenterden town station. The smell of Edward's brewery with its huge dominating chimney stack spouting pleasant fumes hit them as they passed the yard at the back of the pub piled high with hundreds of casks and barrels.

'Look at that pile, they must produce thousands of gallons,' said an amazed Tom.

They walked down a slight hill past pastures and a cemetery and arrived at the station. They went into the small booking hall, but it was empty, so they walked straight out onto the platform. A man in his early fifties and wearing a smart uniform approached them.

Edwin said, 'You must be Mr. Taunt the stationmaster.'

'I am, and how can I help you gentleman?' said Arthur Taunt.

'I am Detective Sergeant Fowle, and this is Detective Constable Luck. We are from the Kent County Constabulary and would like to ask you a few questions if we may.'

'Certainly, but is there anything wrong?'

'No, no, we are hoping you and your staff can help us with some inquiries.'

'I will if I can,' volunteered Arthur.

'Nice tidy station you have here by the way,' he commented looking down the line, 'and a beautiful view over the countryside.'

'Thank you. It's all relatively new so hasn't had time to get grubby.'

'First though it would be helpful if you give us some information about the train line so we can orientate ourselves.'

'Well, it's only a short twenty-seven-mile branch line, but has quite a few stops, some just halts where you have to wave the train down. It only fully opened five years ago and originally ended at the old Tenterden station a couple of miles down the line but two years ago the line was extended to Headcorn.'

'Is that where it joins the main line?'

'That's correct. You walk across the platform and can get to Maidstone, London or Ashford and further afield.'

'And the same at the other end at Robertsbridge?'

'Yes. Again, cross over and you can get to Hastings or London.'

'So, it's quite a slow journey then?'

'It is, that,' laughed Mr Taunt.

'To business then. We are trying to trace the movements of some Algerian pedlars who have been in the town recently and wondered if you had caught sight of them last Friday or Saturday?'

'I've heard about what happened Sunday afternoon. Terrible thing. Did they do it?'

'At the moment we have them in custody while we investigate, that's why we are trying to track their movements.'

'Well let me see. I remember them well, what with wearing the red hats and tassels and all. We do not get many foreigners around here. I remember two of them arriving lunch time Friday. They came into the booking hall and the younger of the two asked if he could leave a package here. I said of course if he paid for a cloakroom ticket which he did. I watched them from the door walking up the hill to the high street chatting,'

'Can you describe them?'

'The young one was quite short and looked just a boy but quite strong looking. The older one was a bit taller with a small moustache like the lad's.'

'Did you see them again?'

'Yes, it was strange. Friday evening, must have been about seven thirty just after the evening train from Robertsbridge arrived three of them came in. The original two plus another one, late thirties I'd say, who was quite tall with a large moustache curled at the ends. Hadn't seen him before. The young one asked if he could remove some mats from the package he had left earlier to sell in the town, which he did. I saw no more of them that night and went off duty at 9pm and closed the station.'

'Did you get a good look at the third one or see where he came from?' asked Edwin

'I presumed he got off the train and met up with the others. He wavered in the doorway and didn't enter the booking office, but I could see his face distinctly.'

'So, you could identify him if we got you to look at the four in custody?'

'I am sure I could if he is one of them.'

'They didn't come back that evening?' asked Tom.

'Definitely not, but I was on duty for the early train from Robertsbridge Saturday morning which arrived at 8.35am and the short young lad jumped off, ran up to me and asked for his parcel. He gave me the ticket and jumped back on the train.'

'How did he seem?'

'He was in a terrible hurry, but he asked me the fare to Ashford.'

'Thank you Mr Taunt that is extremely helpful. We will get on the next train if we may as we have people to interview along the line.'

'Help yourself. Would you like a cup of tea while you wait. I can soon rustle up one. It will be a while yet for the next train.'

'That would be very good of you.'

As Arthur Taunt walked away Edwin said to Tom, 'Well we have established Iddir, Ben Ali and possibly the one named Salem were all in town Friday evening.'

They wandered the platform taking in the view with cups in hand until the train to Robertsbridge pulled in and they got on. As they settled down to enjoy the wonderful countryside on both sides, the guard came into the carriage to check their tickets and they showed their warrant cards.

'Police eh, I hope I am not in trouble?' joked the guard.

'No, but you might be able to help us with our inquiries,' said Edwin. 'We are trying to find information about the movements of some foreign hawkers on Friday and Saturday.'

'You mean the ones with the red hats?' the guard immediately commented.

'That's right. Did you have any dealings with them? Sorry, what is your name, sir?'

'It's George Parish and yes I saw a lot of them.'

'Really, how so?'

'I was the guard on the Friday evening 6.37pm train from Robertsbridge and two of them were on it. I booked the taller one with the funny moustache to Tenterden and the other, who I hadn't seen before, to Headcorn. The one with the moustache alighted at Tenterden about 7.25pm and the other got off at Headcorn and changed for Ashford.

'Would you recognise both of them if we arranged for you to look at them?'

'I reckon so.'

'The one returning to Ashford must have been the fourth one of the band who is now also in the area,' said Tom.

'Is that the only time you saw them?' continued Edwin.

'No. On Saturday morning I was guard on the 6.32am train from Tenterden to Robertsbridge and there were no foreigners on it, but on the return train at 7.42am to Headcorn I saw another young foreigner get on the train with no ticket and booked him to Ashford.'

'Was he one of those you saw the previous night?'

'No, he was a different one.'

'Could you describe him?'

'Well, he was a tiny little fella with dark curly hair and a moustache. I remember he gave me a half-crown coin and I gave him six pence change. He got off at Tenterden in a hurry with a cloakroom ticket in his hand, spoke to the stationmaster and retrieved a parcel. He then jumped back on the train. He looked really rough as if he had not washed that morning.'

'Again, would you be able to point him out if we arranged it?'

'Certainly. You might want to speak to my son Henry. He's a goods clerk and travels on the train sorting the freight, I'll get him for you at the next stop.'

'Thank you Mr. Parish, you have been immensely helpful.'

A few minutes later a young lad no more than 15 years old came tentatively into the carriage.

'Hello Henry, nice to meet you,' welcomed Edwin. 'Your father said you might be able to help us?'

'I'll try,' he said.

'Did you see the two foreign men on the train Friday night?'

'Yes. I saw them and the older one spoke to me asking if I was travelling on the train as well or something like that. He was difficult to understand. The young one had a new blue cap with a star badge pinned on the front of it and he showed it to me.'

'Did you see the older one get off?'

'Yes he got off at Tenterden and I saw him walking towards the exit. I've seen him before in Robertsbridge.'

'Thank you, Henry.'

They settled down again as the train trundled on passing across country lanes and various stations and halts just made of sleepers and earth banks.

'Look at that Tom,' he said pointing out of the window.

Tom looked out and could see an almost complete castle perched on a hill with its high walls and turrets all intact.

'We must be pulling into Bodiam. Not too many stops now to Robertsbridge thank goodness.'

'It's a slow old service I must admit.'

When they got to Robertsbridge they found a large station which formed a junction with the main line. Edwin wanted to find William Hodges the signalman who apparently had information for them.

'Have you ever been in a signal box before?' he asked Tom.

'Can't say I have.'

'Nor, have I. It should be interesting.'

The signal box was situated at the end of the platform, so they walked down the end slope and the few yards to the bottom of the wooden steps that led up to the box. The door above them opened and a man shouted down to them.

'Sorry gents you are not allowed up here.'

Tom shouted up, 'It's all right we are the police and would like a few minutes of your time if it's convenient?'

'In that case you better come up.'

They climbed the stairs and entered a room with a panoramic view of the railway lines. It was full of levers and a variety of other equipment. Edwin asked Mr Hodges about his sightings of the suspects.

'We know these men as they have been in the town for a few weeks and it's only a small community so you couldn't miss them. There were two of them staying up at the Railway Tavern. On Friday evening I saw one of them sitting on the grass bank opposite my box at about 5.15pm but he wasn't one of those lodging here. He was quite young not much more than a boy and dressed similar to the others with a red sash round his waist. I lost sight of him at about 6.15pm and thought he had gone back into the village but then I spotted him a bit later with Salem on the platform. I have seen Salem often and the other one who calls himself Oily for some reason. They have tried to sell stuff to us when they first got here but have given up now. It's mainly rubbish. They got on the 6.37pm to Tenterden and Headcorn which left at 6.42pm.'

'Did they have anything with them?'

'No, they didn't, which was strange as they always had a bundle of things to sell. I did notice something being passed between them but could not make out what is was. Do you fancy a brew. I was just about to make one.'

'Thank you Mr Hodges, but we just had one kindly made by the stationmaster at Tenterden.'

'Old Arthur makes a good cup.'

'He certainly does,' agreed Edwin. 'Good day to you.' Edwin walked back down the steps and turning to Tom said, 'Time to go to the Railway Tavern and see what they have to say.'

'Sounds good to me,' replied Tom.

They walked the few hundred yards to the public house and went in where they were greeted by a stern looking lady behind the bar.

'Are you Mrs Allen, the landlady by any chance?' asked Edwin.

'I am. Who are you? By the looks of you I'd say the police,' she said defensively.

'And you'd be right. We are detectives from the Kent County Constabulary and wanted to ask you a few questions about two of your lodgers.'

'We're not happy with you lot. It's not right coming in here in the middle of the night breaking down doors and causing a fuss. It's not good for our reputation.'

'Yes, well I'm sorry about that but needs must as they say.'

'What you want to know anyway?' she asked rather belligerently.

'Could you tell us anything about their movements on Friday and Saturday last week particularly Saturday morning?' Edwin asked patiently.

'Quite a lot actually as there were a lot of comings and goings I can tell you. I remember Salem and Oily both left in the afternoon on Friday but said they were not selling which wasn't normal. I got the impression something was up.'

'Why so?'

'Well, another one named Belkacem had come here all the way from Ashford and asked to see Salem. He seemed agitated, worried even, said it was urgent he spoke to him. I said he wasn't here, but they usually returned to have their tea. He said to me, "don't tell the little one I have been," meaning Oily which seemed odd and then he left, but he came back an hour later still looking for him.'

'And when did Salem get back?'

'Oily and him came back about six and while they were sitting having their tea I overheard them talking. Salem said, "me no business tonight," which was unusual as they often worked in the evenings. Oily said, "me do business in Netherfield" which is some five miles from here. They went out at about 6.30pm or so. Oily took his wares with him to sell, but Salem took nothing, and I think they split up.'

'And when did they return?'

'I didn't hear or see Salem come in, but I know he didn't sleep here that night as I heard Oily come back at midnight alone and he had breakfast on his own next morning. He then went out saying he was going to the station in search of Salem as he was worried about him. That was about 8.30am. Half an hour or so later I spotted Salem through the window on his own coming from the direction of Bodiam heading down the street. It could have been a bit earlier. He was wet through as it had rained a lot during the night, and he looked tired and weary. Salem came back here with Oily soon after. Oily seemed concerned about him and made him some breakfast, but he couldn't eat much. He sat by the fire and took his coat off and dried it. I told him he ought to change, and he agreed and went to his room saying he had walked from Wadhurst.'

'Anything else?'

'He was acting strange, and he locked himself in the room. He was in there a long time and so Oily went to see if he was alright but couldn't get in which surprised and obviously worried him. They didn't usually lock the door. Eventually he came out and I noticed he had changed wearing grey trousers instead of the dark ones. He had something wrapped in a roll of newspaper about eight or nine inches long and as big around as my wrist. They then went out together and came back an hour later without the package. All day he acted restless and didn't eat much of his meals.'

'Thank you for your time Mrs Allen and again I'm sorry for the intrusion,' said Edwin placatingly.

As they walked towards the station, Edward Bashford hailed them from his butchers shop and asked what was happening with Salem and Oily.

'You knew the suspects did you Mr Bashford?' asked Edwin.

'Yes, well I see a lot of what goes on standing in the doorway when I'm not busy. They've been living in the town for about three weeks now, strange but nice lads. They often bought meat and steaks from me to cook for themselves'

'Did you ever speak to them?'

'Oh yes quite often. They came in the shop several times and we had a bit of a chat. Got to know 'em a bit and knew their names, that kind of thing. Felt a bit sorry for them what with the lack of English and being in a foreign land.'

'Were they ever any trouble?'

'Not that I know of.'

'Did you see them last Friday by any chance?'

'Well yes now you mention it. I saw the one called Belkacem go up to the entrance of their lodging at about 4pm on Friday, probably visiting the others as he didn't lodge there'

'Was that all?'

'No. A little before 8am Saturday morning Oily came into the shop looking for Salem. Asked if I'd seen him as he hadn't come home Friday night. I said no but suggested he might have gone to Hastings to see his brother. He said he'd go down the station and enquire and went off. Then soon after I spotted Salem walking down the road from the direction of Bodiam. I called out to him and said good morning. Told him Oily was worried about him and had gone to the station. I said to him, "where have you been. You are all wet through." He replied, "Me have walked from Wadhurst." I said you'll catch cold. Go change your things and I offered him a cup of tea, but he said "Me won't wait, me will go to station and find Oily. Me will be back and have tea." Ten minutes later he came back with Oily and had the tea.'

'Thank you Mr Bashford you have been very informative.'

'Tell you what. See that lady on the other side of the road, that's Alice Seabrook. She knows everything that goes on in the village if you know what I mean,' he informed the officers with a wink, 'she might be able to help you.'

Edwin and Tom quickly crossed the road to the lady who was walking away carrying her wicker shopping basket.

'Mrs Seabrook?' Edwin called out and the woman stopped and turned round. 'Could we have a word please. We are police officers.'

'Well of course,' replied the startled woman.

'Nothing to worry about. We are trying to establish the movements of the foreign gentlemen who were staying in the tavern.'

'You mean Salem and Oily.'

'That's right. You knew them?'

'Yes, we often had a little chat. It helped them with their English.'

'We are interested if you saw them on Friday or Saturday.'

'Let me see. I saw them on Friday afternoon. Must have been 5.30pm or so heading up from the station but I didn't speak to them. Oh, and I met Salem in the street on Saturday morning. He looked in a right state, all wet through and muddy. I asked if there was anything wrong and he said he had just walked back from Wadhurst and mumbled something about bed bugs. All most strange.'

Edwin and Tom continued on to the station and got on the next train back to Tenterden. On the way they reviewed what they had learned.

'So, what do you reckon on this morning's work, Tom?'

'I'd say we have established Salem was definitely in Tenterden Friday evening, didn't come back to his lodgings that night, turned up in a state Saturday morning and broke his usual routine. Also, that Oily is probably not involved.'

'Well summed up Tom and I totally agree. One thing though.'

'What's that?' asked Tom.

'Why on earth is Meznow called Oily?'

*

Not long after returning to Tenterden Edwin announced to Tom, 'We need to get over to Ashford and have a word with the staff at the Star Inn.'

'But we have only just got back from Robertsbridge.'

'You know what they say, no rest for the wicked.'

He marched out of the police station followed by Tom. It was a forty-minute carriage ride to Ashford. The Star Inn was positioned on East Hill a back street not far from the centre of town. It didn't have a particularly good reputation but provided the type of cheap basic accommodation that the hawkers preferred. George Skinner was the landlord and was happy to speak with them enjoying the limelight.

'When did these men first arrive?'

'I remember the young one Belkacem coming on Tuesday night last week and asking for lodging for three of them. I think they had been staying in Hastings for quite a while. He said they would move in at 10am on Wednesday. I had a room with a double and a single bed and they took it. The next day Belkacem returned with Iddir and Ben Ali and they all slept here. They only brought a box, a bag and some table cloths in a bundle with them.'

'Did they all seem to get on?'

'I saw them laughing together on Thursday afternoon and I overheard Iddir call Ben Ali a bloody b.......... a couple of times, but they seemed happy. Belkacem asked if I could find room for two more and I said, oh yes. He said Ben Ali and Iddir would fetch the others from Robertsbridge on the Friday, but that never happened.'

'Can you describe their movements on Friday?'

'They all went out in the morning, and they started walking up East Hill together, but Belkacem turned and said "Me not going away. Me coming back."'

'And did he?' asked Tom.

'Yes, Belkacem returned at ten past eleven and he had to knock, as it was past hours. I let him in The other two did not return that night.'

'When did you see Ben Ali next?'

'He returned on the following morning. I was standing by the front door at about 10am and saw him coming down East Hill from the direction of the station. He was wet through, and I remember his boots were very wet and the top of his trousers and boots were covered with grass and buttercup fragment's as if he had been out in the grass.'

'What was he wearing?'

'Dark trousers I think and a dark guernsey and a red Fez. He had some rugs and table cloths over his shoulder.'

'Did you speak to him?'

' Yes, I said "Good morning. Where is your uncle" and he replied, "I have my business and my uncle has his." He didn't seem happy.'

'What did he do next?'

'He walked through the bar and into the kitchen where Belkacem was sitting. I went in a few minutes later and saw the two of them changing boots. I asked why they were doing that, and Ben Ali said, "My feet sore and wet. His boots dry." They then went out and an hour or so later came back and I noticed they'd had their hair cut. They laughed that it cost them 4 shillings. They looked quite different. They were both wearing blue caps with stars on them but changed into red Fez's.'

'Thank you Mr. Skinner. I understand one of your bar staff had dealings with them. Is that correct?'

'Yes, Joe saw them that morning. I'll go and get him.'

Joseph Brown was hovering by the bar and was also eager to give his version of events.

'I saw Ben Ali in the kitchen sometime between 9 and 10am. I noticed his boots were smothered in mud, grass and buttercups. When I came in, he put his hands in his pockets and pulled out a handful of silver and he gave me one penny to get a glass of beer for myself. I had not seen him with such money before as Iddir always paid. I asked him where his uncle was and he said, "I don't know."

'Did you ever see Ben Ali and the uncle quarrel or fight?'

'I can't say I did, but they did chatter loudly and do a lot of gesturing.'

'Anything else you can think of that might be relevant?'

'They swapped hats which was odd and went out and had a haircut. Ali was very restless on Saturday and Sunday. He seemed as if he didn't know what to do with himself and even refused meals.'

'Anything else?'

'Yes, something strange happened.'

'What was that?'

'Belkacem was cleaning his black boots and Ben Ali asked to use his blacking and he used it on his.'

'What was strange about that?'

'Well Ben Ali's boots were brown.'

'Thank you, Joe.'

They walked out of the pub and Edwin turned to Tom and said, 'Well, well. The staff at the Star Inn have just given Belkacem an alibi.'

'Looks as though we are down to just two suspects now,' exclaimed Tom.

*

The Reverend John Jarvis, the vicar of St Michaels church was approached about where and how the body of Iddir should be respectfully interred as he was of the Mohamedian faith. There was no family living in the country and returning the body to Algeria was not practical. After discussion the Reverend offered burial in the churchyard on the proviso there would be no ceremony. On Wednesday 22 June Iddir aged 35 was buried in a corner of consecrated ground in St Michaels churchyard only a few hundred yards from where he was brutally murdered. There was no headstone to mark the spot.

*

The prison wagon outside Tenterden Police Station. There was always an excited crowd of onlookers wanting to see the prisoners being escorted into the court room upstairs. [Daily Mirror, 21 June 1905]

Ferat Ben Ali being escorted by Detective Constable Luck and another officer from the police wagon into Court. [Daily Mirror, 20 June 1905].

6 :

Inquests, Court Hearings and a Confession

Their day was nowhere near over as they had to attend the inquest that evening at the small Victorian St. Michaels school next to the church. They had been working nonstop all day but were pleased with their progress. Tom had the job of escorting the prisoners in a carriage the mile and a half to the school from the police station, but Ben Ali caused a fuss and flatly refused to attend the inquest. Rather than drag him manacled there, he was left behind as his presence wasn't vital at that stage.

There was a small group of fascinated and excited onlookers outside the police station to watch the other one, Belkacem, being walked the few steps into the carriage and there was another small gathering to see him being led into the school. All wanted to see what the possible murderers looked like. They were probably disappointed to see just one frightened teenager and not a hardened criminal.

When Tom escorted the young Belkacem into the schoolroom he was visibly shaking, crying and looked as though he was in "abject terror and despair." He was in such a state that after a short while the Major allowed his removal on compassionate grounds. It was only that morning that the teenager had been shown the mutilated and putrid body of his uncle and now with little English at his command and no understanding of what was happening and why he was there, it was no wonder he was in such a state.

The members of the jury consisted entirely of volunteers from the hamlet who were all friends and close neighbours living within a half mile of each other and so the atmosphere was somewhat jovial more like a get together. Some individuals on the jury were strangely also witnesses in the case. They became more solemn once sworn in and began to realise the gravity of the situation. They were a representative group of age and occupation.

The jury consisted of John Appleyard the 58-year-old schoolmaster, Percy Ripley, a 44-year-old wheelwright, William Milton the village baker, Ambrose Fuggle, a 55-year-old farm worker, William Roberts senior, a 55-year-old gardener and his 34-year-old son William Roberts junior, a bricklayer, George Whybourne a 35-year-old farmhand and Frank Watts, a 20-year-old assistant engineer. The others were 44-year-old Frederick Dunster, another gardener, Frederick Sherwood, a 27-year-old coachman, J Hart, George Reeves, a 32-year-old Farm labourer, H George and Samuel Hayward, the village blacksmith who acted as the foreman.

The Major opened the inquest, and as promised it was a very quick affair being just a formality to comply with the requirement of beginning the inquest within forty-eight hours. Edwin stood and confirmed that he was present in the Crown Inn stable at 9.30am that morning when the body had been identified by Daka Belkacem as that of his uncle Hadj ou Iddir and he then detailed the injuries for the record.

David Collins also gave his account of how he discovered the body and Constable Byerley explained what he had seen. The blood-stained clothing belonging to Ben Ali had been sent to Dr. Sir Thomas Stevenson at Guys Hospital in London for forensic examination. He was a Home Office scientific analyst and expert witness, who was knighted in 1904. He figured in many celebrated murder cases and his investigations were viewed as being of "outstanding skill and patience, and his evidence was scrupulous, succinct, calm and lucid." His services were in great demand across the country. The inquest was then adjourned until Tuesday 27June pending further investigation and interviewing any witnesses who might come forward. The prisoners were remanded in custody.

This first inquest was the beginning of a long succession of hearings and magistrates trials which must have been a real test of endurance for the four defendants. They were at a terrible disadvantage as they only spoke pidgin English and initially there was no interpreter to help them.

As it was a Coroner's court they had no legal representation either and relied on the Clerk, a Joseph Mace, and the Coroner to try and explain the procedure as they went along. The prisoners were given opportunity to challenge or ask questions of the witnesses but obviously they had no knowledge of the judicial system in England and didn't understand when anyone tried to explain it to them. Both the Major and the Clerk did their best but at nearly all these hearings the frustration of the defendants would boil over resulting in outbursts, unrest and disorder.

They had to listen to the same evidence being repeated over and over again and it is no wonder that they began to get despondent and in the case of Salem frustrated and volatile. Despite all the histrionics the warders reported that there seemed little resentment between them in the cells, and the prisoners were "as jolly as possible together."

After the inquest Edwin turned to Tom and said, 'Well thank goodness that's all over for today. When you have dropped the prisoner back, it's time for us to get back to Maidstone and get what rest we can. It's going to be another long day tomorrow at the magistrate's court.

*

The first hearing before the Tenterden magistrates was at 10am on Tuesday morning 20 June held in the tiny police court above the police station. The legal system at the time called for the local magistrates to try the case first and dependent on the outcome refer it to the County Assizes court if required. Ferat Mohamed Ben Ali and Daka Belkacem were brought up from the cells while Frank Salem and Meznow Mohamed were transported over from Cranbrook police station as there was not enough room in either police station for that many occupants. The usual gathering of townsfolk had collected outside the police station to get a glimpse of the arrival of the two prisoners from Cranbrook, and the town had a real buzz about it. Edwin and Tom had made the journey back from Maidstone. Having got passed the throng of reporters Edwin and Tom took their seats. The last thing they really wanted was to be stuck in court all morning.

Edwin was being pestered by reporters who were arriving in Tenterden representing local and London newspapers. Edwin had no time for the press, believing they never wrote their reports accurately but embellished and sensationalised everything to garner more readers, so he never gave interviews. The press had got hold of the story early on Sunday evening soon after the body was found and were immediately attracted to the incident by its savage and peculiar nature with the band of "foreigners" being involved. These early reports soon after the story broke on the Monday morning were rushed and had many errors including the nationality of the arrested men, their names, the date and time of the murder and the way the body was discovered.

By Tuesday there were even more correspondents present, including the Press Association representative who was eager to syndicate the story to their member provincial newspapers across the U.K. The reports reached the furthest corners of the British Isles within days. *The Dundee Courier* and *Aberdeen Press* were two of many who covered it in Scotland, the *Jersey Evening Post* in the Channel Islands, the *Londonderry Sentinel* and *Belfast Newsletter* in Ireland, the *London Evening Standard* and *The Globe* in the capital. Amazingly there were literally hundreds of newspapers following the story.

St Michaels and Tenterden were receiving recognition by the nation unfortunately for all the wrong reasons. St. Michaels was dragged from its obscurity and because few people outside of the County had heard of the place, the press began headlining the story as the better known "Tenterden Murder" with headlines such as "Tragedy at Tenterden, Foreigner Murdered" and "A Mahometan Murdered at Tenterden, Four Arrests." Most people had no idea what a Mahometan was or that they were followers of Muhammad the Islamic prophet, but the term was often used generally in old English to denote a Muslim. Some modern-day Muslims consider the term offensive because it suggests they worship Mohammed rather than Allah.

The four bewildered and dejected looking Algerians were lined up in the dock, all charged with being concerned in the murder of Hadj ou Iddir. They presented what was called in newspaper articles as a "rather pathetic sight" as they nervously awaited the proceedings. It was the first time that onlookers had seen the band all together. They were dressed in European attire except for Belkacem who wore his favoured fez and scarlet sash. This initial hearing like the inquest was again only a brief affair with evidence put forward that the motive was robbery, a theory that dogged all the hearings and trial to the exclusion of anything else.

Constable Byerley described what he saw in Churchfield, 'I was called to the scene by Collins and Blackman and was shown the body. There, with his face turned up to the sky, was who I now know to be Hadj ou Iddir, with his head almost cut off, his skull fractured and stabbed all over the body.' His graphic testimony caused a few gasps. Mrs Appleyard the school master's wife gave evidence that she only saw Ben Ali with one other man walking towards the scene of the murder and partially identified Salem as the other person on the Friday night. This caused an uproar among the four defendants who excitedly whispered together in French for a lengthy period resulting in Salem shouting, 'You want to kill me! It was my brother. He looks like me!'

The railway employees and staff of the Star Inn in Ashford interviewed by Edwin and Tom testified to the movements of the men on the night before the murder. These investigations had shown that Meznow "Oily" Mohammed had not been anywhere near the scene of the murder and so the justices acquitted him of any offences and discharged him, but he was remanded in custody under a Coroners warrant to attend the next inquest hearing.

The other defendants were remanded again until Thursday 29 June to give the police time to investigate and find more witnesses and to await the results of the examination of some blood-stained clothing found on Ben Ali. The magistrates asked for the Treasury to accept the case due to its complex nature. Treasury Counsel was a government team of specialist advocates who prosecuted the most serious and complex cases in the country, a procedure which changed in 1908 and today the Crown Prosecution Service instruct and advise the prosecuting teams.

This meant that the Algerians were going to be faced with the full force of the law, but probably didn't realise it. It was finally decided that in fairness to the defendants an interpreter was desperately required, and a Mr Charles Pembo, the official interpreter for the County of London and Middlesex was engaged and travelled down for later hearings. Although proceedings were later translated, the defendants only received an abridged version of what was being said due to time constraints which was still frustrating for the accused. At the end of the hearing the prisoners were transferred to Maidstone prison where they remained throughout all the further hearings and were allowed to communicate with the French consul.

*

With the proceedings finished Edwin and Tom went downstairs into the police station where Sergeant Sales called them over.

'The Doc has dropped off his post mortem results for you. It's on the desk in the office.'

'Good old Doctor Joyce. Got that to us in good time. Let's see Tom what he has got to say.' Edwin picked up the report and perused it. 'He says that the state of the deceased's brain showed that Iddir was alive when the blows were struck, and the heart was acting vigorously.

The small amount of blood from the wound in the throat points to the fact that the deceased was already dead when the throat was cut. So, in other words the blows killed him, and the throat cutting was unnecessary.'

'The killer must have panicked and wasn't sure he was already dead.'

'Let's see. What else has he to say. The deceased had evidently made no attempt to defend himself and as the left ear escaped injury he has concluded that he was lying on his side when hit and was struck from behind.'

'Iddir was obviously asleep, and the killer crept up on him,' commented Tom.

'But why were they sleeping in the field in the first place?'

'Too late to find anywhere else?'

'Perhaps. Anyway, Doctor Joyce has also examined some of Salem's property and found bloodstains on his knife which appears to have been recently sharpened. He has also examined Ben Ali's vest and handkerchief and there's a small quantity of blood on them, but not on his knife. And finally, the hair clotted with blood on the bludgeon corresponds with that of the murdered man.'

'Doesn't look good for Ben Ali and Salem then.'

*

Later that afternoon Edwin asked Sergeant Sales, to give him the cherrywood cudgel used in the murder and turned to Tom Luck.

'Tom, I'm going out for a while so can you keep an eye on things.'

'Where are you going?' he queried.

'For a walk in the woods, that's where.'

'A walk in the woods,' Tom repeated, 'whatever for?'

'You'll see, won't be long.' And with that he walked out the door swinging the heavy stick in his hand.

He turned left and headed up the High Street past the Eight Bells pub on the right and then the old Woolpack coaching inn on the left and admired the ancient Town Hall next door. He continued along the road and past the New Inn. It crossed his mind what a splendid number of drinking houses they had in the town, nearly a dozen he had been told, and all visited by his suspects. He headed out of town towards St. Michaels, again a route the suspects had used several times that Friday evening, and eventually reached the bench positioned at a junction with Beacon Oak road. He was there because the witness named Gwendoline Cole, who lived at number two, had passed Iddir and Ben Ali a couple of times sitting there. On the second occasion she had seen one of them coming out of the wood further up the road possibly holding something behind his back. Another witness, George Bassett, had seen Ben Ali at 11pm Friday night carrying a freshly cut "bat" behind his back and swinging it when he spoke to them outside the Fat Ox which is situated halfway between Tenterden and St. Michaels. Edwin had this gut feeling that Ben Ali might have been doing more than relieving himself in the bushes. He located the copse and orchard she had mentioned, and he pushed his way in and began slowly examining the lower branches of the trees, one by one.

He thought he was probably on a fool's errand, but it would be good to tie up a loose end and it was refreshing to be out on his own in the summer air. After a while he was beginning to think he was wasting his time but then spotted a freshly broken end of a branch. He stepped over to it and placed the end of the "bat" alongside the end of the broken branch and they matched. He went back to the police station feeling triumphant and told the bemused Tom. He later asked Constable Byerley to return to the wood and remove a section of the broken branch from the tree so that the match could be displayed in court.

7:

Detective Edwin Fowle Analyses the Case

By Wednesday 21 June a steady stream of witnesses were coming forward to help with the inquiries and these all aided in confirming the whereabouts of the deceased and his four compatriots during the hours before and after the murder. A rather macabre daily ritual was taking place when most of the male witnesses were taken to see the body to identify him as the one they had seen.

James Brown, barman of the Star Inn in Ashford was quoted as saying "I knew it was him before I had seen his face because I saw his boots had been mended with wire to keep the sole and upper together." Once most of the early witness statements had been gathered, analysed and sorted by Edwin, he had managed to put together a pretty clear picture of the circumstances on Friday and Saturday, so he called a meeting for 8am to appraise every one of the findings so far. Edwin's father along with Tom, Sergeant Sales and his constables were all present. It was protocol for Edwin to keep the superintendents of whichever division he was working in appraised and in this instant this was easy being that he was his father and easily contactable. He had borrowed a chalk board from the infant school just up the road and began the meeting by going over the witness statements.

'These hawkers certainly seemed to have made an impact on the town in such a short time as it appears everyone and their dog had a sighting of them on that Friday and Saturday,' he began.

'Well, they were hardly inconspicuous were they?' commented Tom which caused some laughter.

'And they tried selling their damn mats to anybody they came across,' pitched in the sergeant.

'Which probably means the robbery might not have been planned otherwise surely you would have come up with a more furtive plan wouldn't you?' questioned the superintendent.

'Yes, you could be right. We must have fifty odd witness statements now, so their high profile has helped us no end to virtually pinpoint where they all were throughout the day and evening, except for a few unconfirmed identifications. So, what we need to do is try and go over their movements and come to some conclusion of who was in the vicinity at the time and could have done it,' summed up Edwin. 'Let's get the easy ones out of the way first,' he continued, 'Daka Belkacem now seems to have a solid alibi thanks to the staff at the Star Inn who have him tucked up in bed from about midnight Friday night. Meznow Mohammed didn't stray from the Railway Tavern or go to Tenterden, so he has been acquitted. This means we are left with either or both of the other two or we are looking for a totally different suspect.'

'From what we have got so far I think we have the right suspects,' commented the superintendent, 'I cannot see who else would have any motive.'

'The whereabouts of Iddir and Ben Ali are pretty clear on Friday afternoon. They were wandering all over Tenterden and St. Michaels and were seen by many people. Gwendoline Cole saw Ben Ali and Iddir sitting on the bench at Beacon Oak Road twice in the afternoon and saw Ben Ali coming out of the wood possibly with a stick. They even tried to sell their items to her. Mrs Applegate also saw them on the bench on two occasions,' said Edwin.

'And Bill Roberts said they passed his allotment in Grange Road, St Michaels at 4pm and his friend called out "here comes the Russians,"' added Tom.

'Now our problem is with Frank Salem. He continually denies that he has ever been to Tenterden and at every opportunity has made a point of telling anybody he meets that he was in Wadhurst. He complains that he gets mixed up with his brother because they look

79

like each other, which is somewhat absurd as he is much taller, stouter and has that ridiculous moustache. But Mr Hodges the signalman at Robertsbridge saw him and Belkacem get on the 6.37pm train. And at Tenterden the stationmaster and another railway worker, Mr Parish, saw him get off and meet up with Iddir and Ben Ali. They collected their wares from the booking office which they had left there earlier in the day.'

'So, we now can safely say that Salem, Iddir and Ben Ali were definitely in the town from 7.15pm onwards and that Belkacem went on to Headcorn and changed trains for Ashford. Which means he definitely lied when he said he had never been to Tenterden,' summed up Tom.

'Correct. Now Iddir must have split up from Ben Ali and Salem sometime between 6pm and 7.30pm because Iddir was seen drinking from the village pump alone in St Michaels at 8pm' continued Edwin.

'That would be right as it takes about a half hour to walk there from the bench they were seen on earlier,' commented the sergeant.

'And Iddir then went into the Crown to sell his wares,' said Byerley.

'Then we have sightings of Ben Ali alone in the town at 8.15pm thanks to several witnesses, but he must have re-joined Salem just after that by prearrangement or chance in town and went into the Eight Bells and Woolpack,' pointed out Tom.

'We have no sightings of Salem during that short period, do we?' commented the superintendent.

'No, it gets vague as we run out of sightings of either of them until 10.45pm which is a real problem,' lamented Edwin.

'Ben Ali was back in the Eight Bells at 10.45pm. So, when did Ben Ali and Salem part company and where was Salem between then and the early hours of next morning. Was he the mystery man spotted by George Bassett lying in the hedge dead to the world asleep?' asked Tom.

'George Bassett wasn't a hundred percent sure and that's the problem. Friday night after closing time the town probably had several who never made it home,' suggested Edwin.

'Very true. But it doesn't seem right to me. I don't think it was Salem,' Tom added.

'I agree,' said Edwin, 'And what about the three mysterious men, one carrying something seen by Frank Mitchell the butcher on his way home from Biddenden, near the scene of the murder?'

'A bit of a coincidence if it wasn't Iddir, Salem and Ben Ali,' the superintendent pointed out.

'But again, we have no proof, only supposition.'

'We now know that neither Ben Ali or Salem went to their lodgings on Friday night and appear to have been wandering around in the dark and rain all night because we have sightings of them all over the countryside,' stated Edwin.

'Which means Ben Ali and Salem had to meet up somewhere in the early hours. It can't have been by chance surely,' queried Tom.

'I agree with all of you. So, it looks as though from the evidence and their behaviour on Saturday morning they were both involved, but let's just go over their movements. It seems that they left the scene, and both headed for Robertsbridge. I cannot understand why they didn't head for Ashford. It was closer and a straight run and Ben Ali had lodgings there. He said he had lost his bearings which is unlikely as to get to Robertsbridge involves going back through Tenterden which he must have realised was the wrong direction. Mr Simmons said he saw them at the Junction Inn at Sandhurst early, asking the way to Robertsbridge.'

'We have another witness saying Ben Ali and Salem passed her gate about 5.30am and Salem asked the way to Bodiam, and a local postman passed them walking towards there.'

'Time wise that fits with them getting to the Junction Inn.'

'What I don't entirely understand is what they did immediately after leaving the Junction Inn.'

'Another though saw both of them walking through Salehurst on the way to Robertsbridge but only Salem was seen arriving about 8am.'

'I think they were both in a panic and didn't know where to go or what to do,' added Tom.

'I believe they went their separate ways at this point. Ben Ali must have decided not to continue to Robertsbridge with Salem but turned back and went to Bodiam to catch the early train,' stated the superintendent.

'I agree. The landlord's daughter at the Castle Hotel in Bodiam says only Ben Ali came into the pub for a drink and she didn't see Salem. She insists Ben Ali then rushed to the station to try and catch a train to Robertsbridge, but for some reason changed his mind and decided to take the Headcorn train and then back to his Ashford lodgings.' stated Edwin.

'And Salem wandered on to Robertsbridge on his own. But why not catch a train at Bodiam?' Tom pondered.

'Who knows.'

'Strange also that Ben Ali took the time to jump of the train at Tenterden and collect his wares. Not the action you would think of someone who had brutally murdered someone a few hours earlier,' said the superintendent.

'A good point,' agreed Edwin.

'Again we have a period where we are not sure what they did but I don't think it really matters.'

'So, the murder took place around 1am and we reckon it's a fourteen mile walk to Robertsbridge which would have taken them say six to seven hours with rest stops and getting lost and mostly in the dark.'

'Salem is seen by witnesses arriving in Robertsbridge at about 8.30am, which fits, and he went back to his lodgings and locked himself in and changed his clothes. Ben Ali got on the train either at Bodiam, but we have no witness to that, and then from there to

Ashford arriving at the Star Inn about 10 or 11am, It's all possible time wise,'

'It works for me. So, what with blood on their clothes and the money shared in their pockets I think gentlemen that we have our murderers,' announced Edwin.

'I told you the motive was robbery,' repeated Tom.

*

The adjourned inquest of the week before was resumed at 11am on Tuesday 27 June in the Tenterden police station courtroom with Major Murton again presiding. The four defendants had been brought over again from the austere Maidstone prison in the prison wagon, a black coach pulled by a single black horse giving it a sombre appearance like a hearse. It had side windows and a rear window with curtains that could be drawn across to give the prisoners some privacy. They were always in the company of warders. Whenever they were brought to the town the word went round of their expected arrival and a large group of residents would gather to get a glimpse of them. It was rare for the town to have such excitement, and no one wanted to miss out. Edwin and Tom were always there to escort them into the court.

This was the third time the defendants had been hauled in to hear the same evidence. During the proceedings Ferat Ben Ali, according to a reporter, "cut a melancholy figure" but the others were all in an agitated and excitable state and were incessantly and loudly chattering between themselves. They were oblivious to Joseph Mace and the Major's efforts to quieten them down. Even though an interpreter was now on hand, communication was still fraught with the defendants getting frustrated and finding it difficult to comprehend why they were there and what was going on. On this occasion their main frustration was that they wanted to say something but were not being allowed to do so.

It took several minutes for the Major, Joseph Mace and the warders to get their attention and eventually some order was restored, but within minutes Salem began to shout and "seemed unable to control himself." The Major then lost his patience with him and ordered the warders to remove him from the court and take him down to the holding cells.

Meznow Mohamed who had been calm and quiet up to this point suddenly asked to see the photograph of Iddir that had been used in evidence. It was a rather horrific photograph showing the shocking injuries sustained. On receiving it Meznow kissed it passionately and then collapsed in a fit on the floor. Several people went to his assistance and the Major asked for his removal as well, and for medical help to be summoned.

Following all this drama the inquest got underway. All the witnesses that had been involved in finding the body, examining it and investigating the murder were called and these included Dr Joyce, Dr Matthews, Edwin, Superintendent Thomas Fowle, Charlie Fox, David Collins and Constable Byerley. In total seventeen witnesses were examined at length with the proceedings lasting all day from 11am to 6.20pm when the case was adjourned yet again until Friday 30 June at 11.30am to await more forensic evidence.

*

Next day at 10am the magistrates hearing was continued, and all four prisoners were charged on suspicion of being concerned in the murder of Hadj ou Iddir, but it was going to be a rewarding day for Meznow Mohamed. The hearing continued for most the day with 18 witnesses being called, most of them the same as those who gave evidence at the inquest the day before. They were all questioned at length by the Crown solicitor, Mr F.G. Frayling. At the end of all the testimony he addressed the judge and stated that the evidence against Meznow Mohamed, also known as Oily, was insufficient to justify a remand "as no evidence beyond circumstantial testimony of a vague nature had been forthcoming." The Borough Justices agreed and so he was discharged. Meznow's delight at hearing the news through Mr Pembo was short lived though, when the court advised him he was to still remain in custody under the coroner's warrant until the next inquest hearing.

Mr Frayling stated that the evidence against Belkacem was also weak, but he believed it was sufficient to justify a remand. The magistrates agreed and he was held in custody along with the other two.

Belkacem whispered something to Pembo who translated it, 'Mr Belkacem says he would rather have his throat cut here and now rather than go back to Maidstone prison. He does not like it there. He asks not to be returned.' While Pembo spoke, Belkacem emphasised his request by drawing his finger across his throat. The case was adjourned to Monday 3 July.

*

The final coroner hearing was resumed on Friday 30 June at 11am and proved to be a long trying day which at times was almost riotous. Seventeen witnesses gave evidence to the movements of the defendants on the day of the murder and the following morning and were examined by the Coroner. The three charged men Ferat Mohamed Ben Ali, Daka Belkacem, and Frank Salem, were standing together guarded by warders from Maidstone prison. Their presence was to prove helpful as all three defendants appeared to be in an agitated state. Only Meznow Mohamed appeared calm as he had been exonerated. He was only present in case he was needed to give evidence as a witness. He stood away from the other three. A rather harassed Charles Pembo again functioned as interpreter.

There was already a sense of excitement in the court, but this turned into pandemonium when Major Murton reopened the inquest. When the proceedings began all the prisoners started shouting in broken English and French indicating they all wanted to speak. Salem insisted he should be the first, but he was told to be quiet. The Major who had already had problems keeping them under control in the previous hearings had to repeatedly tell them to be quiet and valiantly tried to restore order. He rebuked and warned them on several occasions, but they ignored him. They were all overly excited, except for Belkacem who was rather withdrawn. Ben Ali and Salem then had an intense argument in French and started pushing and shoving each other and it looked as though they were squaring up.

The warders were asked to intervene and calm them and Belkacem helped them by speaking to his compatriots and pleading with them. Warders were then placed between the two men to keep them apart, but they continued to argue and so the Coroner told the warders to physically restrain them if they appeared to be going to "go for each other." When order was restored Salem was allowed to speak but immediately became animated and shouted in broken English, *"I am looking for the man that killed my brother. I would kill myself. I would kill him* (pointing to Ben Ali*). I don't care. He has killed my brother, and he is kill me. I like to dead myself."*

The Major sternly told Salem to be quiet, but he remained on edge. Through the interpreter, who was looking quite bewildered at this point, Ben Ali asked to make a confession. Mr Pembo passed on his request to the coroner. When asked after the trial Charles Pembo stated "I cannot say whether he wished to make a statement that first day. It may have been so. He was excited before he started writing it and while he was doing it he calmed down. He and Frank were both excited. They both wanted to make a statement first. I advised Salem not to."

The Major replied, 'Could you inform the defendant that he should not make a confession unless he really wants to as this is not a trial.'

The interpreter advised Ben Ali of what the coroner had said but he insisted, 'I want to make confession.'

He advised him again, 'I am not entirely happy about this, Mr Pembo could you please advise the defendant that anything he says now could be used at his trial?'

Mr Pembo translated the Coroner's advice to Ben Ali. Having listened, he shouted, 'I understand what I am doing, and I am happy to repeat it at my trial.'

'In that case, please continue.'

At this point Salem, who had been leaning up against the wall glaring at Ben Ali and visibly shaking, sat on the floor, put his head in his hands and started crying. The warders tried to get him up, but he shrugged them off. The Major motioned to leave him be, but he then started slapping his face quite violently and loudly shouting '*Oh dear! Oh dear!*' The proceedings had to be halted because of the disruption he was causing. He was eventually calmed down and the prisoners were then provided with a seat during the remainder of the inquiry.

Ben Ali then stood and read out his confession in French to an eerily quiet room and it was dramatically interpreted by Charles Pembo phrase by phrase as follows:

'I admit that I killed the deceased, Hadj ou Iddir, and Salem was not with me. I was quite by myself. The reason why I did that on Friday, l came from Ashford with him, (Iddir) we stopped at Tenterden, and we left our goods at the parcel office at the railway station. Shortly after he asked me to take a small parcel out of those goods in order to sell them during the evening. When I had taken the goods he required we started together, and then we divided among us the goods

87

that were to be sold. In the evening, after we sold all our goods I asked where are we going to sleep.

"He said you come with me, and I shall find a place to sleep in."

When we were near the church (St. Michael's) he told me:

"Come just here and we shall sleep here in the field."

I retorted that I was very tired and required better accommodation. I went to sleep, nevertheless. Towards one o'clock in the morning I felt somewhat chilly and awoke.

[It was at this point that Ben Ali emotionally described how Iddir allegedly attempted to sexually assault him, but his exact words appear not to have been transcribed or possibly censored by both the press and court as the only reference on record is that Ben Ali "went on to suggest that the deceased had endeavoured to assault him." None of the newspaper reports from correspondents in the court dwelled on the point either.]

I turned round, pulled my knife, and cut his throat as he was lying down, and gave him another stab. Afterwards I seized the piece of stick that was lying between the two of us and I gave him two heavy blows on the head. I wished to state this on the first day, but I was not allowed to speak.

As soon as I realised what I had done, I started to go away. I wished to make for Ashford, but evidently I mistook the way, because after walking all the night in the rain which soaked me, I found myself in Bodiam in the morning. When I arrived at Bodiam I met Salem, who is the brother of the deceased. He called me three times, and I would not reply to him because I was afraid that he may kill me. When he approached me he said, "Your face is quite white, and you are all in a tremble, what, is the matter with you?"

I replied: "I have lost my way and have been in the rain all night and I am cold."

He asked me whether I wished to have some drink, and I said, "Yes I would like some rum."

He paid for some rum for me. I then asked him to show me the way to Ashford, saying I wished to go there.

He asked me, "Where is my brother." and I said "Your brother is all right. He is at Ashford with Belkacem."

When I had done with him I came to Tenterden by train. I took my parcel from the railway office, and I went to Ashford.

You have heard the reason which has forced me to commit such a deed. If the British law allows men to be turned into women by whomsoever to do so, then I had better turn a woman myself. If you had seen such a thing among English people I don't know what the English would do. That man attempted to commit a deed on my person. I admit that I killed him in revenge and am ready to forfeit my head for what I have done. I am also willing to kill the brother, so that I might be sentenced for two murders instead of one. I am afraid of nothing.'

After this dramatic confession, the courtroom was deathly silent as everyone was trying to process what they had just heard. It was an unexpected turn of affairs. The inquest was then adjourned to be resumed in the morning.

Edwin, Tom and Superintendent Fowle, had been in the courtroom observing all the mayhem and came out bewildered.

'What on earth just happened in there,' queried the superintendent.

'I have no idea,' replied Edwin

'It was quite a surprise to me as well,' put in a stunned Tom.

Edwin said, 'I thought Ben Ali's solicitor was going for a not guilty.'

'Fat chance of that now he has confessed,' answered the superintendent.

'Why would Ben Ali make a confession at the inquest and not the trial, or make a confession at all for that matter?'

'Perhaps he doesn't understand the English legal system,' suggested Edwin.

'Sometimes I have difficulty as well,' laughed the superintendent.

'Yes, but his confession is totally at odds with what we know from witnesses. All that information in the confession was basically a lie,' said Tom.

'Indeed. We know Salem was with him in Tenterden or in the vicinity, but for some unfathomable reason he is covering for him,' replied Edwin.

'But why sacrifice his life to safeguard Salem? There seems to be no love lost between them?'

'His description of the actual murder is false as we know that Iddir was killed by the blow on the head not the cut throat.'

'Yes, and he said he met up with Salem in Bodiam, but we know they were together before then, and anyway what would he be doing in Bodiam in the middle of the night. And where did they get the rum, certainly not from the Castle pub,' explained Tom.

'It's all very strange,' agreed Edwin.

*

Next morning on the Saturday, the Coroner summed up and sent the jury out to deliberate in private. After just fifteen minutes they returned with solemn faces.

'Have you come to a verdict Mr foreman on which you all agree?'

'We have sir,' replied Mr Hayward.

'And it is?'

'Wilful murder sir against Frank Salem, Ferat Mohamed Ben Ali and Daka Belkacem.'

'Thank you.'

Superintendent Fowle then charged Ben Ali, Salem and Belkacem with the wilful murder of Hadj ou Iddir.

'So, what happens next?' pondered Tom.

The superintendent replied, 'On Monday the Tenterden justices will have no choice but to commit Ben Ali for trial at the next County Assizes.'

'And we'll be back in there going through it all again. I can't wait,' moaned Tom.

*

The three prisoners charged with the murder were brought up before the magistrates on Monday 3 July and poor Meznow Mohamed who had been acquitted was again present. They must have wondered when all the legal proceedings were going to end as they were tired of being transported between Maidstone prison and Tenterden. All the evidence given previously was repeated including the confession, probably to the frustration of the prisoners who had heard it several times before. Dr Matthews and Dr. Joyce repeated their evidence. When they gave details of Salem's knife with the traces of blood stains on it, Ben Ali shouted, 'That's not the knife. I killed the man and I have thrown away the knife I did it with, that's not the knife.'

The prosecution concluded their case and immediately Salem made a long rambling statement, the contents of which was bizarre. He tried to convince the court that he had met a stranger at Robertsbridge station who looked just like him and Salem had helped him by paying for his ticket. It was this man who had travelled on the train to Tenterden. Therefore, it was not him on the train, so he was never in Tenterden that Friday evening. It was his naïve attempt to concoct an alibi for his whereabouts despite the evidence against the claim. During this long statement Joseph Mace interrupted him several times asking him to speed up his oration which only caused him to lose his temper not for the first time at such proceedings. Eventually he shouted in English, 'Do what you like. I can't tell my story. I can't speak. Do what you like.'

He then refused to take any more part in the proceedings and also refused to sign his statement. With Mr Pembo translating, the quiet Belkacem also said he wouldn't speak but would wait until the Assizes trial. Then Salem started shouting again in French which Pembo translated as, 'Ben Ali kill my brother. Me borrow knife. Kill Ben Ali. Kill myself.'

Then Ben Ali expressed his readiness to kill Salem, and everything got out of hand again. Ben Ali asked for police protection insisting they should keep them apart as he was afraid that either he should kill Salem or Salem would kill him. He repeated, however, that he was afraid of nothing.

Despite these "bloodthirsty" outbursts by all the prisoners, the magistrates didn't feel Salem was a threat to Ben Ali or vice versa as during the proceedings neither of them had attempted to raise a hand to each other, even though they were not manacled and only had Belkacem standing between them.

Mr Frayling, prosecuting, addressed the bench, 'Your honours, it is my opinion that there is insufficient evidence to show that Mr Belkacem had anything to do with this tragic incident or was anywhere near the vicinity, therefore I would ask that he is not committed for trial. I truly wish he had made a statement today. I would though ask that the other two defendants are committed for trial.'

But the justices having had a short, whispered discussion disagreed and all three were committed to appear at the upcoming Summer Assizes in Maidstone beginning on Monday the 10 July. Until 1972, when they were abolished and replaced by a single permanent Crown Court in the UK, most counties had periodical courts for civil and criminal cases presided over by judges from London. Two or more judges travelled a circuit visiting major towns three times a year and there were seven circuits. The courts were reserved for the most serious cases directed to them by local County courts or Magistrate courts.

The prisoners took the verdict very quietly, but Mezron Mohamed, who had been acquitted was obviously relieved. At the end of the hearing, he saluted the magistrates and expressed his gratitude for his release and his admiration for England and offered his services to the British army, which brought some levity to the court.

Tenterden bobby outside the police station and lock up where the hearings took place in the small courtroom on the first floor. [Tenterden archive]

Major C Murton (left), Det. Sgt Fowle and Superintendent Fowle (in uniform) discussing the case outside Tenterden police station. [Daily Mirror 21st. June 1905]

8:

The Trial

The 1905 Summer Assizes for the County of Kent began in Maidstone on Monday 10 July, with 63-year-old Justice Sir Reginald More Bray, a high-profile High Court Judge from London presiding. Earlier that morning the judge had attended divine service at the parish Church of All Saints, as was his habit, probably to gain guidance for what was going to be trying list of cases. He entered the chamber; everyone rose and were then seated. Before starting proceedings, he made a point of commenting, 'that both the criminal and civic business is one of the heaviest experienced at these Assizes and I am sorry to see so very heavy a calendar of crimes of a serious nature.' There were in fact 56 prisoners awaiting trial including four for murder, six for manslaughter, six for arson and two for rape. It was obvious from the start that Sir Bray was not a happy judge due to the workload.

The Grand Jury was sworn in and had been selected mainly from the landed gentry and the class regarded as Gentleman. They had to number at least 14 and no more than 23 and the names of those summoned were called and sworn in. Although Judge Bray announced that the Tenterden murder was the "most important" on the agenda he didn't begin the case until later in the week

All three defendants were present and were asked how they wished to plead and with Mr Pembo translating, Belkacem and Salem pleaded not guilty and Ben Ali, guilty. At this point Mr Waterlow, Ben Ali's counsel, interjected on behalf of him to say, 'If it pleases your Lordship I would like to ask that Ben Ali's plea be taken as one of not guilty.'

His Lordship replied, 'Due to the circumstances, I would concur as I do not believe that the prisoner entirely understands his position in this matter.'

'Thank you my lord.'

The judge then began to summarise the facts for the Grand jury to deliberate on and come to a verdict. This was required under the law at the time so that they could confirm probable cause or enough evidence to believe the defendants were guilty to allow the case to be heard. He would inform them of the charge and draw their attention to the facts and give explanations before the jury retired to a room to decide on whether there were sufficient grounds to put the accused on trial. A minimum of 12 had to be in agreement and they would declare a "true bill" for a trial to go ahead or "not a true bill" if they believed their was not enough evidence.

Those elected were Mr C Whitehead (foreman), Captain Moore, Colonel Lock, Colonel Grubb, Captain Palliser, Captain Down, Surgeon-General Planck, Mr T Collyer-Collyer Ferguson, Mr D Wentworth-Reeve, Mr C Powell, Mr R Locke, Mr T Powell, Mr A Waring, Mr A Hardcastle, Mr H Smith, Mr F Monckton, Mr Montagu Cook, Mr T Jobson, Mr Bevan, Mr A Boosey, Mr Laurie and Mr H Hohler. Twenty-two men of obvious breeding, and no women of course, who were to decide the fate of the three itinerant Algerian pedlars.

The five men had been living together for some two months and on June 13 they separated. Three of them, Belkacem, Ben Ali and the deceased were staying at Ashford and the other prisoner Frank Salem staying at Robertsbridge. The murder took place on the night of the 16 or 17 June and according to the depositions, Ben Ali was seen on two or three occasions during the night with the deceased. Ben Ali has, moreover, confessed to the crime and made an excuse for his conduct which is no excuse in law. You, the grand jury therefore should have no difficulty in coming to a conclusion in respect of Ben Ali.

Regarding Belkacem, he undoubtedly was at Ashford on the night named. I believe he arrived there at 9.00pm or 10.00pm and he certainly did not leave the town until seven or eight in the morning. The case against this prisoner seems rather weak. But it is not easy for me to tell from the depositions exactly what the evidence might be.

As to he was seen with Ben Ali several times during the night and in the early morning I'm beyond all doubt he was not at his lodgings at Robertsbridge. There was also the fact that a handkerchief and one or two other articles belonging to him were found to have blood upon them. I believe that you the grand jury will probably find that there was a sufficient prime facie case against Salem.

Ben Ali when he made his confession alleged that Salem, who was the deceased man's brother, took no part in the murder but you must not place too much trust in this statement, because it might be that Ben Ali was trying to shield him.'

The grand jury then retired to discuss the judge's summary of the case and returned with what was called a true bill, meaning they had decided there was enough evidence to try them. The judge then committed all three for trial.

*

The murder trial was finally opened on Thursday 13 July at 10 am. Once again Edwin and Tom were present at court to witness the final chapter of the case. At least they didn't have to travel all the way to Tenterden, but just down the road from Maidstone police station. They were about to discover the results of their hard work and that of the team. For the last few weeks, they had been busy on other cases assigned to them which thankfully did not include murders. They were to sit all day reliving all the evidence they had collected including their own.

Tom asked, 'What do you reckon, one or both?'

'I have to admit I am worried about a Salem conviction. We never did quite get the evidence to prove he took part in the murder, only circumstantial.'

'Surely the jury will see he must have been part of it.'

'You know juries Tom; you can never second guess them.'

Just then the three prisoners were led up to the dock and Edwin looked over at Daka Belkacem, Ferat Mohamed Ben Ali and Frank Salem standing mournfully with their eyes downcast. It was difficult not to feel sorry for the two teenagers who had come all the way from Algeria for a better life and ended up being charged for murder. With that the clerk announced, 'All rise,' and Judge Bray swept in, and the case commenced.

Mr Boxall. KC along with Mr G F. Hohler prosecuted for the Crown. Each defendant had their own defence counsel who were sitting together. Mr Weigall represented Frank Salem, Mr Waterlow for Ferat Ben Ali and Mr. Guthome Hardy represented Belkacem.

It was a packed courtroom as the murder case had generated a great deal of interest across the County and had been covered and syndicated across the whole of the U.K. in great detail. A correspondent commented that Belkacem and Ben Ali acted with their usual sangfroid as though trying to distance themselves from what was happening. Frank Salem on the other hand, who had always been the most volatile at all the previous hearings, appeared extremely dejected burying his head in his hands.

Mr Boxall then got up to open the case for the prosecution and faced the jury.

'Gentlemen of the jury, I will try and be as brief as possible with my opening remarks, but as you will see this is an extremely complicated case involving three defendants. You will, during the trial, be confronted with a lot of technical evidence in regard to timings of movements of the three accused leading up to and after the alleged murder. The prisoners and the deceased man were itinerant Algerians travelling throughout the counties of Kent and Sussex selling rugs, embroideries and jewellery. The three prisoners along with a young lad named Mezrou Mohamed, nicknamed "Oily" were apparently under the command of the murdered man. Hadj ou Iddir procured the stock for them to sell and also allowed them money for their expenses. You will discover that the men frequently quarrelled over money.'

He then went on to describe how the body was discovered and the injuries before describing the movements of the accused and then:

'There seems little doubt that Belkacem was at Ashford at the time the deed was committed, and the probability is that when the court arrives at the evidence upon that point I will apply for Belkacem's dismissal. With Frank Salem and Ben Ali however, it is different. They were seen, as abundant evidence will show, in the company of the murdered man in Tenterden at a late hour on the evening the murder was probably committed. The prosecution will show that on that night, Iddir sold most of his goods at the Crown Inn leaving that place with something like two pounds in his pockets. Yet when the body was searched only four shillings was found upon him.

Ben Ali in his confession has put forward the defence that the deceased, during the night had assaulted him by trying to commit unnatural acts upon him and in revenge he committed the crime. But the prosecution finds this story difficult to accept and even if true does not justify committing murder. The prosecution will show that the motive was that of robbery.'

*

The first witness called to the stand was William Lucas Turner, the Tenterden Borough surveyor who had been asked to draw up a map to pinpoint the position of all the towns and villages and other locations that were going to be mentioned in evidence. Also, the timings and the distances between different points and the railway links. These all had a great relevance to the case because of the way the accused had used the railway extensively to travel as well as walking long distances, particularly in the early hours after the murder. These included where the body was found, the jubilee bench, the Fat Ox, the wood where the cudgel was obtained and many others. Mr Turner positioned it so that it could be seen by everyone and explained it. At this stage, the proceedings became very technical in character, with his Lordship, Counsel and witnesses discussing mileage and the time it took to walk between certain points.

The judge then directed that the evidence would be heard, and the rest of the day was taken up with a procession of witnesses. After each witness had given evidence, Mr Pembo, gave a short translation to the three defendants who "listened as men who had heard it many times before."

First up was David Collins, who explained how he and his companion discovered the body in Churchfield. He described the position of the murdered man and the obvious injuries. At this point the exhibit of the bludgeon was shown to the court and David formally identified it as the one he had seen by the body.

PC Byerley was next to the stand dressed smartly in his uniform and he retold how he was called to the scene by the previous witness. He described the injuries in graphic detail from his notebook and gave a description of the clothing, the bloodstained ground close to the head and all the trampled grass around the body.

A nervous Charlie Fox was called and said he noticed the man lying in the long grass and thought he was a drunk and ran away. Then the evidence began tracing the whereabouts of all the defendants before and after the murder. First up was the lodging house landlady Mary Ferrari from Hastings.

Mr Hohler asked: 'Mrs Ferrari , when did the defendants first come and stay in your lodging house?'

Mrs Ferrari explained that during their stay at her house they paid on time and the "old gentleman" was the boss who the others always paid their earnings to. She did cause some humour in the court when asked by Hohler how old she thought the old gentleman was and she replied, 'about 35 or 40, I should say'. Mr Hohler then asked: 'Did you ever hear them quarrelling?'

'I didn't hear them quarrel, but other lodgers complained about the noise late at night when they came in.'

'So, they didn't get on?

'Well, I wouldn't say that, but the old man often had his meals alone.'

'Why did he have his meals alone?'

'Well, sometimes the others were out all day.'

The courtroom erupted in more laughter.

'When did they leave your house for good?'

'Salem and Ben Ali left something like three weeks before Iddir and the other two.'

'Thank you Mrs Ferrari , you have been most illuminating.'

Mrs. Ferrari was then crossed examined about the meals and noise and stated that they were very talkative and gesticulating with their arms rather than arguing. They sometimes cooked for themselves and lived very frugally.

Jane Rebecca Allen, wife of the landlord of the Railway Tavern in Robertsbridge was up next. She pointed out Frank Salem and Meznow as the two staying with her. She explained they used to go out after tea every evening selling and came back late.

Mr Boxall asked the witness, 'on the Friday in question did you see either of them go out?'

'Yes, they both left in the afternoon but said they were not selling. I got the impression something was going on.'

'Why is that?'

'Well, the other one, Belkacem came to the house and asked to see Frank. I told him that they would be back at tea time. He said to me, "don't tell the little one I have been" and he then left, but he came back an hour later still trying to find Frank.'

'When did he get back?'

'They came back for their tea, and I overheard them talking. Frank said, "me no business tonight" and Oily (Meznow) said "me do business in Netherfield." They went out at 6pm or so and Oily took his wares to sell but Salem took nothing.'

'And when did they return?'

'I heard Oily come back at midnight and he had breakfast on his own. He then went out and headed for the station about 8.30am. I saw Frank pass by alone from the direction of Bodiam and at about 9am Oily and Salem came into the tavern.'

'And then what happened?' prompted Mr Boxall.

'Oily seemed concerned about him and made him some breakfast, but he couldn't eat much. Frank was wet through and looked tired and weary. He sat by the fire and took his coat off and dried it. I told him he ought to change, and he agreed and went to change saying he had walked from Wadhurst. He was very restless.'

'Can you remember what he was wearing?'

'When he came in he was wearing dark trousers, but he changed into grey ones and had a dark waistcoat and jacket and a grey cap. He was wearing the grey cap when he went out on Friday.'

'Have you seen the dark trousers since?'

'I have not.'

'What happened next?' Urged Mr Boxall.

'Frank was acting strange and went to his bedroom and fastened himself in. He was in there a long time and so Oily went to see if he was all right but couldn't get in. I had not known them lock the door before so Oily was surprised. Eventually he came out with something wrapped in a roll of newspaper about eight or nine inches long and as big around as my wrist. They then went out together and came back an hour later without the parcel. All day he acted strange, was restless and didn't eat much of his meals.'

Mr. Gathorne-Hardy then stood and asked, 'When Belkacem came and told you he wanted to see Frank and did not want to see Oily, he made no secret about it. He was perfectly open in his manner, is that right?'

'Oh, yes sir.'

'Had Ben Ali ever visited before?'

'Yes sir. Ben Ali had come once before with the deceased, and they had attracted a good deal of attention around Robertsbridge dressed in their Fez's and sashes. It was unusual to see foreigners in the village. I've only had one before last Christmas although I've heard folk say they have seen others in the district.'

'How did Salem and Oily seem to get on?'

'Salem was much older and seemed to be the master of Oily.'

Mrs Allen was cross-examined and asked if Salem could have come back unnoticed late that night.

'It would be quite impossible for anyone to come in without seeing them. You have to go through the kitchen to get to the bedroom.'

Next was George Skinner, the landlord of the Star Inn in Ashford. At this point the proceedings became a little farcical because try as he might, George was unable to pronounce the prisoners' names which caused a great deal of laughing and snickering from everyone in the court room. Despite many futile attempts his Lordship had to intervene.

'Mr Skinner, I am sorry you are having such difficulty pronouncing the names of the prisoners, but it is important for the record that we know who you are talking about. May I make the suggestion that in order to distinguish them you point and say the man this end, the man at that end and the man in the middle?'

'Yes sir.'

Mr Skinner reiterated that Belkacem was at his premises all the night when the murder took place as he remembered having to unlock the front door for him when he returned at ten past eleven.

'Are you positive that Belkacem returned?' asked the judge.

'Yes sir.'

'Did he to your knowledge go out again?'

'No sir.'

At that juncture, Judge Bray announced that, as far as he could see, there was no case against Belkacem. It had been clearly proved that he was miles away at Ashford and alibied by Mr Skinner at the time the murder must have been committed. He then instructed the jury to retire and find a verdict of not guilty against the prisoner. The jury went to their room and a short while later returned and the foreman announced that they had found the verdict of Not Guilty against Belkacem and the judge instructed he should be released from custody.

While all this was taking place a bemused Belkacem sat awaiting a translation. Mr Pembo turned and told him the good news of his release, and his face gradually brightened, and he smiled. He saluted the judge and exclaimed "Merci!" But then he looked perturbed and asked through Mr Pembo what he should do as he had no money. Superintendent Fowle was in court and stated that he had been caring for the fifth member of the band Meznow Mohamed and he and his wife would be happy to look after Belkacem as well until arrangements could be made for their repatriation. This was gratefully accepted by the court.

Joseph Brown, the barman at the Star Inn, was next and basically collaborated what George Skinner had said. But he added that when he walked into the kitchen Ben Ali put his hands in his pockets and pulled out a handful of silver and gave him one penny to get a glass of beer. He had not seen him with such money before as Iddir always paid. Joseph had asked him where his uncle was and he said, "I don't know." He also confirmed that he had not heard them quarrel.

The next witness called was the star witness Sarah Appleyard, wife of the schoolmaster who was probably the last person to see Iddir alive and had seen them several times during the course of the evening. Gwendoline Cole, the schoolmistress described how she had seen Ben Ali and Iddir on the seat at 5pm and saw Ben Ali come across from the direction of the wood back to the bench but she didn't see anything in Ben Ali's hand.

The staff of the Kent & East Sussex Railway must have been severely depleted on the day of the trial as all those interviewed by Edwin and Tom were present to repeat their sightings .

William Stace, the Eight Bells barman, remembered Ben Ali and Salem entering the public house and having a drink about 8.30pm but Salem suddenly shouted from the dock and interrupted William at this point protesting he wasn't in the Eight Bells or anywhere near, and it was his brother as they looked alike. William was asked again if he was the person with Ben Ali and he nervously replied that he may have made a mistake. William Curtis also placed them in the Eight Bells at the same time.

Albert Edward Bishop, landlord of the Woolpack Inn positively identified Salem and Ben Ali entered his premises on the Friday at 9.15pm. William Reeves, landlord of the Crown Inn said that Iddir came into his pub alone wearing a fez at about 8.30pm selling mats and left at 10.30pm.

George Bassett, a drover of 3 Silver Hill, stated that he was coming home from St Michaels and passed Iddir and another foreigner near the Fat Ox pub at about 11.15pm. He had seen the deceased earlier in the Crown and had left half an hour after him. They went on towards St

Michaels. The shorter one of the two had some rugs and carried a stick behind his back which he kept twiddling about.

Frank Mitchell described how he was driving along the Ashford road in his carriage at about 11.30pm when he passed three foreigners going in the direction of St Michael's Church. He could not identify them in the moonlight as he was high up. One was carrying something over his shoulder.

Abigail Eldridge, postman Edwin Pullen, Ada Roberts of the Castle Inn, butcher Edward Bashford and Herbert Bashford the blacksmith at the Junction Inn all related their sightings of them around the Robertsbridge and Bodiam area during the early hours of Saturday. Alice Seabrook also testified that she had seen Salem and Oily together Friday afternoon at about 5.30pm and again at 8.30am on Saturday in Robertsbridge High Street coming from the station.

This ended the list of witnesses called to determine the movements and whereabouts of the defendants leading up to and after the murder. It was then the turn of the police and expert witnesses.

Major Murton explained that Ben Ali insisted on making a voluntary statement despite warnings from him and the confession was made in French translated by Mr Pembo, and he had written it down. He then showed the court the confession statement and affirmed that Ben Ali wished to take all the blame saying and had said that: *"Iddir had attempted to commit a deed on my person. I admit that I killed him in revenge and I'm ready to forfeit my head for what I have done."*

Superintendent Fowle confirmed that he had charged the defendants with murder on 25th. June and that Detective Sergeant Fowle handed him thirty-five pounds eighteen shillings and six pence found on Salem and eight pound and ten shillings on Ben Ali. He left the stand and was replaced by Edwin, who had been waiting patiently nearly all day to be called and he went through the part he had played in the cautioning and arresting of the defendants. No further evidence was taken that day and the court rose at 6pm with the judge adjourning the case until the morning at 10am .

*

Next morning it was the turn of the other police officers and experts to give their evidence. Tom, who had spent the whole of the previous day waiting to be called and was not amused, gave his evidence along with PC Cloke and PC Apps who described the arrests and finding of the large amounts of money on Salem and Ben Ali.

Then it was time for the medical and scientific evidence to be given and Doctors Matthews and Joyce gave their ghoulish findings confirming that either Salem's or Ben Ali's knife could have been the murder weapon, and that considerable violence must have been used with the bludgeon. Both men agreed that the fractured skull caused the death and that the throat was cut afterwards. They had found some reddish-brown stains on the base of the blade of Salem's knife which proved positive for blood and noted that the blade had been recently sharpened. Ben Ali's jersey had a very small amount of blood stains on the inside of the collar and on the handkerchief, but it appeared to have been recently washed. Ben Ali's knife was clean. This concluded the case for the prosecution. The weight of evidence against them was enormous and damning.

*

Mr Boxall then made his closing argument to the jury.

> 'Gentlemen of the jury, the evidence has clearly established the fact that the deceased was the head of a party of five men and that robbery was the motive for the murder. It has also been shown that the deceased must have had a substantial sum of money upon him immediately before the crime as

107

only four shillings was discovered in his possession after the murder. We have heard from Mr Ben Ali of an alleged assault on his person by the deceased, but there is no evidence of this, and it is fair to believe that this probably did not take place. In regard to Frank Salem, you have heard a detailed description of his movements on the night of the murder and the morning after, compiled from the witnesses here today. It is reasonable to believe that they all point to the conclusion that he took part in the murder. In fact, it appears that he concocted an alibi by claiming he went to Wadhurst in order to account for his movements that evening. It is also significant that £36 was found on him and £8 odd on the other prisoner.'

Mr Waterlow then rose on behalf of Ben Ali.

'I must begin by saying that there is absolutely no evidence to prove that robbery was the motive for the murder. As far as my client and the other prisoner are concerned no one has spoken to having heard quarrels among the five men in regard to money matters. I would like you to bear this important fact in mind when you come to consider the robbery motive adopted by the prosecution. As to the statement made by Ben Ali before the coroner, I would urge you to consider that this was a most extraordinary statement and one which is rarely heard in an English Criminal Court. I submit, subject to his Lordship's direction, that if you believe this statement, then you would be justified in returning a verdict not of murder, but of manslaughter. I also consider that you should accept the prisoner's explanation as to why he committed this act. That the provocation he received was so great that in a frenzy of rage, he attacked the deceased not intending, however, to kill him.'

Salem throughout the trial had been unusually quiet and dejected, but for some reason suddenly lost his composure and threw himself onto the floor as though in a fit. Again, warders went to his assistance and eventually after a few minutes he got to his feet again. With the courtroom settled again Mr. Weigall stood to speak on behalf of his client Salem.

'Before you can convict my client you must be satisfied beyond doubt that he was an active participator in the murder. Even if you think my client is a liar and has not told the whole truth with regards to his movements on the night of the crime and on the following morning you must not necessarily conclude that he assisted in the crime.'

He sat down and all eyes moved to Judge Bray who summed up at great length, but his closing remarks were that:

'Even if Ben Ali's story of the assault on him by Iddir that night was true this would not have been sufficient provocation to justify him in resorting to the extraordinary violence described by the medical men. If the jury found that Ben Ali inflicted the blows which caused the deceased's death then the case is one of murder and not of manslaughter. In the case of the conduct and movements of Frank Salem there is no evidence to prove that the deceased, who were brothers, were on bad terms. Another point in favour of Frank Salem was Ben Ali's statement which stated that Salem took no part in the murder, although you must not rely upon that alone as to his innocence. Against Salem was the fact that he had told an untrue story as to his movements and that a considerable sum of money was found in his possession after the murder.'

The jury was then asked to retire to consider their verdict and after a remarkably short deliberation of half an hour returned to an eerily hushed courtroom. The Clerk then asked the foreman, 'In the matter of Frank Salem, do you find the defendant guilty or not guilty?'

'Not guilty.'

When Charles Pembo confirmed the verdict to Salem he surprisingly received the news with little emotion.

'In that case you are free to go Mr Salem,' instructed the judge.

Frank Salem then left the court room without saying a word. An eager Belkacem was waiting in the lobby and the two enthusiastically embraced. Back in court it was Ben Ali's turn and the Clerk turned to the foreman again.

'And in the matter of Ferat Ben Ali how do you find the defendant, guilty or not guilty?'

'Guilty as charged,' replied the foreman.

There was a loud murmur and some shaking of heads at this declaration. The judge turned to Ben Ali and asked whether he had anything to say on why sentence of death should not be passed upon him. Ben Ali replied, 'I have already told you the law by which I killed that man. I know no other law.'

The court remained hushed and many present looked to the floor as Judge Bray carried out the traditional act of passing the death sentence. He slowly retrieved the black hat and positioned it on his head and put on black gloves before saying:

> The sentence of this court is that you will be taken from here from whence you came and there be kept in close confinement until Tuesday 1 August, and upon that day that you be taken to the place of execution and there hanged by the neck until you are dead. And may God have mercy upon your soul.

When Ben Ali heard about his fate from the lips of the shaken interpreter, he appeared to take it calmly, apart from "some convulsive twitching of his face muscles." Ben Ali without a word stepped steadily from the dock to the cells below.

First page of a three-page letter written by Ferat Ben Ali in prison to his cousin in Algeria after his sentencing stating Salem was involved in the murder with him. [National Archives]

9:
The Day Of Reckoning

After hearing the sentence of death Ben Ali managed to retain his calm demeanour which had characterised him throughout all the acts of the tragedy. He was transported the short distance from the court back to Maidstone prison and initially placed in isolation watched over constantly by warders. He had to contemplate enduring seventeen days patiently awaiting his death. Those who looked after him said he was a model prisoner and the prison Governor stated he was an "exemplary prisoner, remaining incredibly calm and dignified for such a young person alone in a foreign country." Charles Pembo got to know him quite well and said he was "a good French scholar who reads and writes well." He in no way fitted the picture of a young uneducated blood-thirsty person capable of murder.

From all accounts he was of a shy, quiet demeanour and was literate and educated and his youthful age and even younger looks endeared him to his keepers and induced their sympathy. They showed compassion towards him and found him likeable unlike most of the inmates they had to deal with. The staff provided him with whatever they could to fill the hours including finding a supply of French magazines. He did not receive a visit from his compatriots and his family was too far away. He was completely isolated. As the days passed it was obvious that his mental state may have deteriorated into depression.

On the Monday after his trial, he asked for writing paper and pen and sat alone in his cell to write a poignant and somewhat sensational three-page letter to an obviously close cousin in Algeria. In it he asked him to convey his love, sorrow and best wishes to many of his extended family. It was poignant because of his obvious regret and that he was saying a final goodbye. It was sensational because of one sentence midway in the first page of the letter which read, *"nous avont tuer Edhadj ou Iddir. Moi avec Salem."* (We have killed Edhadj ou Iddir. Me with Salem). Why he should have decided to finally tell the truth about Salem's presence and involvement in the murder will always remain unclear. Having been acquitted, Salem could not be retried and so this admission would not have any repercussions for him. Ben Ali appears to have wanted his family to know the truth but gave no indication of why he took the sole blame.

Ben Ali, like his relatives, was a Muslim, or as the newspapers described him, "a follower of the Mohamedian doctrine." The press reported that during his imprisonment, "he had maintained the fatalism characteristic of the Arab to care not whether he lived or died." Efforts were made to find a representative of his faith to give him comfort and guidance, but sadly this was not possible, so the services of a Roman Catholic priest were sought. The Right Reverend Father George Le Bosquet, the rector of the Maidstone mission agreed to help, and Ben Ali received his "kindly attention" on almost daily visits. They appeared to form a rapport and Father Bosquet gave him spiritual aid and comfort and it was reported Ben Ali listened to the priest's words with "interest and even contrition." The *Folkestone Express* wrote that there were rumours that Ben Ali had converted to Catholicism, but these were unfounded, and he never renounced his faith.

While awaiting the day of his demise Ben Ali may have been aware of all the activity by various groups and individuals to obtain clemency for him. This possible chance of a reprieve probably bolstered his morale in the initial period after the trial. Although the local inhabitants of Tenterden and the surrounding area were initially horrified by the murder, and there had been a hue and cry to find and punish the offenders, their attitude mellowed once the facts became clearer and they discovered how young and vulnerable the perpetrator was. The five hawkers had roamed over a large area of South Kent and East Sussex over the previous few months and had become a familiar sight. They caused no trouble and were polite and were befriended by many residents in some of the towns and villages many of which got to know them and their names.

When the death sentence verdict became widely known many were shocked and there was a local groundswell of feeling that Ferat Ben Ali did not deserve to die as it was thought the killing had not been premeditated. It was also probably because he looked so young and innocent, and as the victim hadn't been a local person but "one of his own."

Several groups got together to raise petitions for clemency and many individuals wrote letters, but with just three weeks between sentencing and the execution. there was little time to collect the signatures and to get the petition to the Hon. Akers Douglas, 1st. Viscount Chilston, the Secretary of State. The largest petition, sponsored by the main county newspaper, the Kent Messenger and Maidstone Telegraph managed to obtain 1633 signatures with four days to spare. The newspaper wrote a letter to the Secretary of State on the 24 July asking for clemency and attached the petition with the reasons why. Unfortunately, many letters and petitions didn't arrive at the Home Office until it was too late.

At the time there were many advocates denouncing the death penalty sentence in Maidstone where the hangings were conducted. They believed that although Ben Ali participated in the murder he deserved clemency on the basis of his age, his different beliefs and culture and also the general feeling that it was not just him involved. Some felt the verdict should have been manslaughter and not wilful murder.

The petitions and letters requesting clemency did not appear to have been greeted with much interest or compassion. An internal briefing compiled by Charles Edward Troup, senior clerk to the Secretary of State at the Home Office gives an indication that the Government was not interested in the pleas for clemency even though they accepted the grounds for it. Charles Troup outlined the case for the Secretary of State to make a decision and confirms that the evidence appears:

> to point strongly to the conclusion that the deceased man was murdered by his brother Salem and the prisoner Ben Ali, while possibly a third man Belkacem was privy to the designs before the murder. It is not, however, necessary to examine this evidence in detail, because as the case now stands, Ben Ali was convicted and has confessed, while Salem, though probably equally guilty, has been acquitted.

C.E. Troup also dismisses any possibility of the motive being anything but robbery:

> The only question that remains is what was the motive for the murder? The prisoner, Ben Ali, in his statement before the Coroner, asserted that he and the deceased were sleeping together in a field when he was awakened by the deceased attempting to commit an unnatural offence against him, and that he thereupon cut his throat. There seems no ground for accepting this story, which in itself is improbable, and is contradicted in several points by the evidence, particularly the fact that the clothing of deceased was not disarranged in anyway. And by the medical evidence showing that he was killed by a blow from a bludgeon before his throat was cut. Moreover, there is clear evidence that Salem, whom the prisoner says was not with them, was in their company in Tenterden.

Later in the briefing he makes a reference to Ben Ali's three-page letter, but strangely makes no comment about it: "In a letter, which Ben Ali has written to a cousin while lying under sentence of death, he remarks *"nous avont tuer Edhadj ou Iddir Moi avec Salem."* *(We have killed Edhadj Iddir. Me with Salem).*

Finally, Mr Troup recommends that: "The jury made no recommendation to mercy. The judge has offered no observations in the case and so far as the facts appear at present, there are no grounds for any interference with the capital sentence."

The briefing was dated the 24th. July, several days before most of the petitions arrived at the Home Office making them pointless and showing a decision against clemency had been decided long before. After reading the briefing, the Home Secretary hand wrote a comment at the bottom of the page totally accepting the view of his clerk when he commented, *"I can see no grounds for interfering with the sentence."* It seems there was little consideration given to Ben Ali's fate and as far as the Government was concerned it was all best forgotten about.

In a response to the Kent Messenger newspaper dated 28th. July, it is obvious that the Secretary of State may not have given "careful consideration" to the matter:

Sir,

I am directed by the Secretary of State to say that he has considered the petition forwarded in your letter of yesterday's date on behalf of Ferat Mohamed Ben Ali, now under sentence of death, and that he has given the most careful consideration to all the circumstances of the case; and I am to express to you his regret that he has failed to discover any sufficient ground to justify him in advising his Majesty to interfere with the due course of the law.

I am, sir, your obedient servant

C E Troup.

On Tuesday morning 1 August, only 46 days after Ferat Ben Ali had committed the murder, he was greeting the dawn of his final few hours on earth and his execution by hanging. He woke soon after dawn and unsurprisingly had passed a sleepless night in the condemned cell just yards from the scaffold. The prison was eerily quiet as on execution days all male and female prisoners were confined to their cells. Shortly before 7am he was brought the traditional condemned man's last breakfast of tea, bread and butter. Father Le Bosquet was there when he awoke and stayed with him throughout this traumatic period offering him solace until a few minutes before he was led to the scaffold. He wore his own clothes and continued to wear the traditional bright scarlet waistband sash.

Then the chapel bell began its mournful tolling. The smartly dressed Albert Pierrepoint, the renowned and experienced executioner had spent the previous day inspecting the scaffold. He had also visited Ben Ali and explained the procedure for the following day and taken him to be weighed and his height measured so that he could calculate the required drop precisely. Ben Ali was only 5ft 4½ inches tall and weighed just 121 lbs, so Albert calculated a seven-foot drop. Although only 28-years-old, Albert was the principal executioner in Britain and completed 105 executions between 1901 and 1910 assisted by John Ellis who also became a well-known executioner.

Because of the nationwide coverage of the case, a larger than usual crowd on "hanging mornings" had gathered outside the huge stone walls of Maidstone prison in County Road. Public hangings in front of baying crowds had been banned since 1868 much to the disappointment of many and were now held inside the prison grounds. But this didn't stop large numbers of morbid spectators arriving in the macabre hope of hearing the sound of the trapdoor falling over the pit known as the "drop fall" and to witness the hoisting of the black flag signifying the execution was over.

The hanging was scheduled for 8am and at 7.45am Albert and John Ellis entered the condemned cell and pinioned his arms without a struggle and then escorted him the few yards from the condemned cell to the red doors of the execution shed and the scaffold. He showed no visible sign of emotion and walked the few yards steadily and calmly to stand on the trap door where he began chanting a Muslim prayer in a loud and clear voice in which the name Allah was continually uttered. He climbed up to the gallows and took his position on the drop without help and he looked down at the small group of witnesses in the courtyard below. These were Lieutenant. Lionel Sanders RN, the prison Governor, the Under Sheriff, Dr Hoar the prison medical officer, William Dobson the principal warder, some other warders and two members of the press.

At 7.56am his face was covered, and Albert crouched and tied his legs together while Ellis adjusted the noose round his neck. Both then stepped aside and as the clocks around the town began striking eight, and amid a great hush by the spectators, Albert pulled the lever releasing the heavily weighted trap door and Ben Ali disappeared into the pit to an instantaneous death and a dull thud was just audible outside the prison. Many in the crowd uttered a prayer and crossed themselves.

It had only taken a split second and for the witnesses in the execution shed it was all over before they realised it. According to the *Westminster Gazette*, "he died without a struggle except for the compulsive movement of his body signifying that life was extinct. He died as a Mohammedan." Dr Hoar went into the pit and pronounced that life was extinct. As required by law the body hung there for an hour before being cut down and placed in a plain, unpainted open coffin. As the Black Flag was hoisted and fluttered in the breeze the crowd quietly melted away.

The regulation inquest on the deceased's death which must be held within twenty-four hours of the execution was carried out at 10.15am.

One witness said that his "features were composed but the upper lip was swollen and upturned giving a full view of a fine row of teeth." A reminder perhaps of how young he was. It was a short affair presided over by County Coroner Mr Thomas Buss accompanied by the governor of the prison. A jury was sworn in with a Mr Ratcliffe elected foreman. The prison medical officer Dr. Hoar said he had seen Ben Ali several times while in prison and he was healthy and never complained and that the hanging had been properly conducted causing dislocation of the cerebral vertebrae. Death was instantaneous. It was noted he had lost 4 pounds in weight while confined. His body was buried without any ceremony in the prison grounds.

After Ben Ali was executed, relatives of Iddir were tracked down to a small village in the desert and they requested the return of his money and possessions. At the same time, the relatives of Ben Ali also claimed his possessions including the money. Protracted correspondence and negotiations between the Home Office and Algerian authorities took place that lasted a year before it was decided that Ben Ali's relatives could have the money found on him when he was arrested. This rather sad postscript to the case made a complete mockery of the whole robbery scenario.

There is no record that Salem ever claimed that the money found on him was stolen even though all the evidence pointed to Iddir always holding all the proceeds. Ironically after he was found not guilty these possible ill-gotten gains of thirty-four pounds and ten shillings found on him were given back to him by Superintendent Fowle by order of the court along with his other possessions.

*

6

The case of Ferat Mohamed ben Ali.

This is a case in which the leader of a band of Algerians, who were going about the country selling rugs and embroideries, was murdered by his comrades. His body was found lying in a field near Tenterden on Sunday, July 12, and his four comrades were promptly arrested by the police, two at Ashford and two at Robertsbridge.

The results of the minute inquiries made by the police as to the movements of the four men immediately before and immediately after the murder, as set out in the depositions and the Judge's notes, appear to point strongly to the conclusion that the deceased man was murdered by his brother Salem and the prisoner Ben Ali, while possibly a third man Belkacem was privy to the designs before the murder, but this was certainly not established by the evidence. It is not, however, necessary to examine this evidence in detail, because as the case now stands, Ben Ali was convicted and has confessed that he committed the murder, while Salem, though probably equally guilty, has been acquitted.

The only question that remains is what was the motive for the murder. The prisoner Ben Ali in his statement before the Coroner, asserted that he and the deceased were sleeping together in a field when he was awakened by the deceased attempting to commit an unnatural offence upon him, and that he thereupon cut his throat. There seems no ground for accepting this improbable story which is itself improbable and is contradicted in several points by the evidence, particularly by the fact that the clothing of the deceased was not disarranged in any way and by the medical evidence showing

Internal report for the Home Secretary to decide on clemency with his hand written note:" I see no grounds for interfering with the verdict." [National Archives]

121

that he was killed by a blow from a bludgeon before his throat was cut. Moreover, there is clear evidence that Salem, whom the prisoner says was not with them, was in their company at Tenterden.

If the prisoner's account of the murder be dismissed there remains only the theory that it was committed with a view to robbery. The deceased was the leader of the party, kept the money and paid their expenses (though it appears to be asserted by some of the witnesses that Salem was his partner, the others were certainly subordinate). After the murder Salem was found to be in possession of £38, and Ben Ali, who had previously appeared to have no money, was seen to have plenty and more than £10 was found on him when arrested.

In a letter which Ben Ali has written to a cousin while lying under sentence of death, he says "nous avont "tuer Edhadj ou Iddir Moi avec Salem".

The jury made no recommendation to mercy; the Judge has offered no observations in the case; and so far as the facts appear at present there are no grounds for any interference with the capital sentence.

C.E.T.
24.7.05

I can see no ground for interfering with the sentence.

122

10 :
Afterword

This true story is a murder mystery because we shall never know for certain what happened in Churchfield in the early hours of Saturday 17th. June 1905. Yes, there was a brutal murder, but the motive is unclear. On the one hand we have a sexual assault and on the other a robbery both of which are debatable. Neither do we know whether it was committed by one or two of the suspects and possibly with the knowledge of others.

Ben Ali's stated reason for murdering his "Uncle" was revenge and humiliation caused by the unsolicited attempt at sexual assault on him, but this was brushed aside and never seriously considered. Such an outlandish claim impinged on Edwardian sensibilities. The sensational press of today would have had a field day highlighting this but only one newspaper the *Nottingham Evening Post* mentioned the assault by reporting that "during night he woke up and found the deceased "interfering with him." The stated excuses given for not accepting the claim was that Ben Ali had lied in his confession about cutting his Uncle's throat before bludgeoning him and that Iddir's clothing was not "disarranged," neither of which seem legitimate reasons to ignore the scenario.

The situation though could have been perfectly plausible as Ben Ali could have woken up to find Iddir "interfering with him" and fought him off or even acquiesced. Either way, Iddir would have gone back to his sleeping spot a short distance away "rearranging" his clothes while Ben Ali fumed and got angry and plotted revenge. Waiting until Iddir slept, he could have picked up the stick, crept up and hit him while he was prone on his side. But the act of cutting his throat post mortem is difficult to explain.

Then we have the other situation of whether Salem was present and took part in the murder. The fact that he lied about being in Tenterden was contradicted by a wealth of witnesses. Ben Ali's confession exonerating Salem was riddled with false statements and even the Home Office accepted that Salem, Belkacem and Ben Ali were all privy to the murder and that Salem was present. The blows to Iddir's head were done with great force according to the post mortem and Ben Ali was only a slight figure compared with the heavier and stronger Salem, so it could easily have been him who dealt the fatal blows and or cut the throat. From his performances in court, we know he was of a volatile nature. Salem was also seen in the Railway tavern walking out on Saturday morning with a thin parcel, the shape of a knife, which was disposed of in some way. This could have been the murder weapon.

If the motive was robbery and Iddir did have nearly fifty pounds on his person (a year's wages for a factory worker of the time) and Ben Ali committed the alleged robbery alone, how did most of it end up in Salem's pocket? If Ben Ali had shared it with him, surely he would have been suspicious how Ben Ali had come by it. What makes the robbery motive a little difficult to accept is that there were far better times and places to have committed a robbery and murder than in a dark field in the middle of a village where hundreds of people have seen you.

It never became clear why Ben Ali exonerated Salem and why both of them wanted to make a statement first. At the coroner's inquest he insisted on making his confession before Salem was heard. After the confession Salem refused to make a statement so could it have been he was also going to own up? Having heard Ben Ali plead guilty, Salem might have thought it better for him to take the sole blame. It later transpired that Charles Pembo may have influenced Salem over his wish to make a statement when it was disclosed later that the interpreter stated, "I cannot say whether he (Ben Ali) wished to make a statement that first day. It may have been so. He was excited before he started writing it and while he was doing it he calmed down. He and

Salem were both excited. They both wanted to make a statement first. I advised Salem not to."

We shall never know Salem's intentions but was the show of antipathy between himself and ben Ali just an arranged sham. And could it even be that Ben Ali covered for Salem under some kind of family code or threat to his family back in Algeria. Was it possible that Ben Ali was incredibly magnanimous and believed that it wasn't worth sacrificing two lives when he had the opportunity to take sole responsibility?

Throughout all the press coverage and the court proceedings there was no attempt to get to know these men or their background, particularly Ben Ali. Therefore, it is impossible to assess the social dynamics of the group. The prosecution painted a picture of them quarrelling constantly and of there being antagonism between them and yet most witnesses stated that they never actually quarrelled but that they were excitable, gesticulated constantly, were loud and spoke quickly which being of Arab background are natural traits. This was often misinterpreted as quarrelling. There are many comments that the group seemed to be comfortable with each other and even after being arrested, police officers stated they appeared jolly and got on well while locked in a cell together.

Unfortunately, the trial and its verdicts left a lot of questions unanswered:

- Why did Salem break his routine and go to Tenterden without the intention to sell anything unless there had been a premeditated plan to murder Iddir in some way that night?
- Why was Belkacem in such a hurry to find Salem on that Friday and make such a long journey to Robertsbridge and then straight back to Ashford without staying with them? Could it be he was aware of a plan to murder his Uncle that evening and was trying to stop it?

- Could Salem's possibly blood-stained knife or trousers have been hidden in the wrapped newspaper that Saturday morning and disposed of?
- Why did all of them initially lie about visiting Tenterden when they must have realised this was easily disproved?
- It is difficult to comprehend the behaviour of Ben Ali when instead of trying to flee he calmly collected his wares from the station and carried ion normally.
- Was there a falling out between Salem and Iddir and this was why they group split up in Hastings?
- Where was Salem between 11pm Friday and 1am Saturday? Was he the mystery man lying in the hedge that a witness saw on his way home?
- It was unusual for them not to have previously organised lodging for the night as they had always been methodical about this. So, was the field a random choice or had there been a plan to lure Iddir there if robbery was the real motive.
- And finally we shall never know what they must have talked about during all those hours trudging along the roads in the rain and dark.

There is no way of knowing what Edwin Fowle thought of the verdicts as I have not been able to find any post-trial interviews or press reports. I suspect he was disappointed that he could not obtain enough evidence to place Salem at the scene or implicate him in the murder. He was probably just satisfied he had brought another murderer to justice, but his success was possibly tinged with a thought that one got away.

This thought was compounded no doubt when he heard about the letter Ben Ali had written in prison claiming that they had committed the murder together. It didn't stop him from receiving the plaudits for his handling of the case which he no doubt deserved and a year later, as Constable Byerley and Tom Luck suspected, he was promoted to Inspector.

Many people shook their heads in disbelief when Salem was acquitted and rightly so, but unfortunately, with the execution of Ben Ali, we will never know for sure the full truth of what really happened that moonlit June night.

*

11 :
Edwin Fowle Biography

Edwin Fowle
1872 – 1944
Badge No: 287

Det. Inspector Edwin Fowle on left talking to Supt. Taylor of Sevenoaks Division in 1908 on another case. Courtesy of Alamy Stock Photos.

Edwin Fowle is the central character in this series of books for good reason as he was a much acclaimed and respected police officer in his time with an exemplary and extraordinary career, but like many of his ilk has been forgotten by history. His time as a detective spanned exactly the Edwardian era and during his 42 years and 3 months loyal service to the Kent County Constabulary he was awarded many accolades collecting a police merit star and over twenty commendations.

His police career spanned the reigns of four monarchs, and he experienced the emergence of motor vehicles, extensive train lines, telephones, radio, major advances in forensic science and innovations in policing methods as well as social transformations and changes in criminal behaviour. He seems to have taken all of it in his stride managing to adapt to all the new challenges. He was always viewed as a rising star and rose through the ranks from a lowly constable in October 1890 to Superintendent in charge of his own division in 1911.

He was five feet nine inches tall, broad shouldered and of stout stature with a well-groomed large moustache below a substantial nose. . As a detective he was always smartly dressed, always wearing the fashionable derby hat. He was described as a driven and religious man with a great sense of duty, a somewhat questioning mind and a tenacious nature, perfect attributes for a detective. He was a stickler for correct police procedure and record keeping and his superiors and the judiciary were complimentary for the way he prepared cases for court, few of which failed to get a prosecution

Born in 1872 to Thomas and Margaret in the small village of Preston situated between Canterbury and Ramsgate he became part of a family police dynasty as his father Thomas was also a celebrated Kent policeman who rose to the rank of superintendent and surpassed Edwin by completing 53 years' service. Two of Edwin's three brothers were Kent police officers. His elder brother Thomas rose to the rank of superintendent and his younger brother Ivo was an Inspector and one of his uncles was in the police before becoming a railway detective. They managed to boast three superintendents and an inspector with an unrivalled family service record which spanned an incredible 165 years excluding the uncle.

He worked as a cooper in the village until he was eighteen and able to join the police. During his first six years he was posted to the Kentish towns of Gillingham, Westgate, Dartford, Ightham and Malling where he gained considerable experience. There was no real training at the time, and he learned from his father and other "old hands." From the beginning he was perceived as having a natural aptitude for police work and particularly an ability for investigative work.

So when on the 1 July 1896 the Force had the prescience to establish a detective branch at their Wrens Court headquarters in Maidstone he was immediately picked to become one of the first three detective constables in the history of the force under the supervision of one Detective Sergeant. This tiny unit was responsible for serious crime across the County, and he helped launch and shape this new innovation. He made such an impression that four years later in 1900 he was promoted to First Class Detective Sergeant and was put in charge of the department.

In the next six years he made quite a name for himself becoming one of the most recognised officers across the County although he made every effort to shun the press and publicity and never gave interviews he was ever in the newspapers due to the many headline cases he investigated He was called upon to deal with every known class of crime whether it be murder, fraud, infanticide, robbery, hotel theft, housebreaking or pickpocketing.

His pet hate were all the pick-pocket gangs that frequented Kent which he pursued with a vengeance. One of his attributes was that he never forgot a face. He made a point of knowing them and they soon knew him, some of them to their cost. Such was his fixation that he could recognise all the members of the leading notorious London and

Kent pickpocket gangs. Despite this the criminal fraternity had a wary respect for him and referred to him as "The Terrier."

While a detective between 1900-1911 he collected many commendations and awards. The most memorable being three headline murder cases; known as The Tonbridge murder (1901), The Tenterden Murder (1905) and the Seal Chart Murder (1908). For each one he received a commendation from the Director of Public Prosecutions (DPP) and the Chief Constable and for the Tenterden murder a police Merit Star. These three murders are all part of my *Edwardian Detective Edwin Fowle Series*.

He got married on the 9 November 1910 in St Michaels Church, Beckenham to Annie Sophia Vockins. Edwin remained with the detective department until his promotion on the 20 April 1911 to the rank of superintendent when he moved with his new wife to Sevenoaks to command the Sevenoaks Division, "a post which he held with zeal from that day" until his retirement in December 1932. While in Sevenoaks he was known for his patience and tact and "preventing frayed tempers."

He was a popular officer and familiar to most of the public and highly respected by the judiciary, counsel, solicitors, magistrates and local authorities, coroners and also to many villains. He was also venerated by his men; encouraging them in their recreations especially cricket and rifle shooting and tutored them in first aid. Under his guidance his men played a conspicuous part assisting the injured in the disastrous 1927 Sevenoaks train crash which killed thirteen people. On retirement he remained in Sevenoaks.

He died peacefully aged 73 in Holmesdale Hospital Sevenoaks in 1944 and was buried in Greatness cemetery. At his funeral the vicar spoke of the power by which had lived and served the police force. First there was the sense of duty by which he was always exact, ready and alert to execute his work and secondly there was the maintenance of peace inspired by the source of all power, God.

The funeral was attended by family, dozens of senior officers from across the County, as well as rank and file and a large contingent of local dignitaries, friends, acquaintances and towns folk and even the local RSPCA Inspector.

12 :
List of Real Characters

The high profile of the hawkers allowed police to find many witnesses and to track virtually all the suspect's movements in the days leading up to and after the murder. These for the record are some of the primary ones interviewed and other officials involved in prosecuting the murder.

Jane Rebecca Allen, Landlady of the Railway Tavern, Robertsbridge

Sarah Appleyard of School House, St. Michaels, wife of schoolmaster

Edward Bashford butcher of High Street Robertsbridge who spoke to Salem and Meznow at 8 am on Saturday morning.

George Bassett, a drover, of 3 Silver Hill who met Iddir and Ben Ali outside the Fat Ox at 11 pm on Friday night.

Albert E Bishop landlord of Woolpack Inn, Tenterden.

James Blackman, agricultural labourer of St Michaels, who found the body with David Collins.

Joseph Brown barman at Star Inn who spoke to Ben Ali on Saturday morning.

Gwendoline Cole of 2 Beacon Oak Road, Tenterden saw them sitting on bench and spoke to them.

David Collins, agricultural labourer who found the body.

William Henry Coombe, civil engineer of St Michaels: who saw Ben Ali on the Ashford train on the morning of the 19th

William Curtis of St Michaels Terrace, a labourer, who was in the Eight Bells and later stumbled across a man sleeping in hedge.

Mrs Abigail Eldridge of Ewell House, Ewhurst who spoke to Salem and Ben Ali from her cottage.

Mary Ferrari of 15 East Hill Passage All Saints, Hastings, landlady of lodging house.

Charles James Fox, 13 St Michaels Terrace, who saw the body on Saturday morning but mistook it for a sleeping tramp.

William Charles Hodges, signalman, Robertsbridge station who saw Belkacem meet up with Salem to catch Tenterden train Friday evening.

William Milton, baker of St Michaels who was in the Crown public house with Iddir on Friday night.

Harry Mitchell Tenterden butcher who saw three men on the road just before murder.

Henry Simon Parish, railway goods clerk, saw the prisoners in the train. Salem got out at Tenterden.

George Henry Parish railway guard, Tenterden – said Belkacem and Salem were on the 6.37pm train from Robertsbridge to Tenterden on Friday night.

Edwin Pullen postman of Hawkhurst.

William Reeves, landlord of Crown Inn St Michaels.

Ada Roberts, landlords daughter at Castle Inn Bodiam gave Ben Ali a drink Saturday morning.

William George Roberts, a 34-year-old farm worker of Yew tree Cottages, St Michaels.

Alice Seabrook who saw Salem in Robertsbridge on Friday evening and Saturday morning.

Herbert Simmons, blacksmith who spoke to Salem and Ben Ali in the Junction Inn.

George Skinner Landlord Star Inn Ashford who gave Belkacem, Iddir and Ben Ali lodging

William George Stace, a barman at Eight Bells saw Salem and Ben Ali on Friday evening between 8.30 and 9 having a drink.

Arthur Frank Taunt Station master at Tenterden.

Police

Superintendent Thomas Fowle, the District Superintendent based in Cranbrook and involved in overseeing the investigation and charging prisoners.

Detective Sgt Edwin Fowle, head of Kent County Constabulary detective department based at Wrens Cross police headquarters in Maidstone.

Detective Constable Thomas Luck, member of the Kent County Constabulary detective department.

P.C Mark Edwin Apps of Ashford police who arrested Ben Ali and Belkacem early on Monday morning at the Star Inn.

P.C Albert James Byerley of Tenterden police who was first on the scene and called for help.

P.C Thomas Henry Cloke of Sandhurst police who arrested Salem and Meznow Mohamed at the Railway Tavern, Robertsbridge on the Sunday night.

Others

William Lucas Turner of 1 Beacon Oak Road, Tenterden, a surveyor who drew up a map of the area to show distances and positions of villages and railway to each other for the trial.

Frederick Edwards of St. Michaels, an amateur photographer who took pictures of the body.

Mr C D (Major) Murton District Coroner from Cranbrook.

Mr Joseph Munn Mace, Court Clerk.

Dr Joyce, MD,MRCS

Dr Mathews, MD

Sir Thomas Stevenson, Home Office forensic expert at Guys Hospital, London.

Assizes Court Officials

Prosecution

Mr Boxall KC

Mr G F Hohler

Mr F G Frayling, the instructing Treasury Counsel.

Defending
Mr Gathorne Hardy for Daka Belkacem
Mr Weigall for Frank Salem
Mr Waterlow for Ferat Ben Ali.
Sir Reginald More Bray, The Assizes Judge.
Mr Charles Pembo official interpreter to London County of London and Middlesex.

Selected Bibliography

National Archives, Kew, File HO144/791/130192 Ferat Mohamed Ben Ali.

Documents 130192:/6/9//10/12/14/15/17/18/19

www.britishnewspaperarchive.co.uk

UK Press Online

A Kentish Mystery, Mahometan Murdered, *London Evening Standard*, 20 June 1905, p.9

Tenterden Tragedy, Albanian Murdered in Orchard, *The Daily Mirror*, 21 June 1905, p.11

Terrible Discovery at Tenterden, *Kent & Sussex Courier*, 23 June 1905, p.3

Murder Mystery, Four Algerian Mat Pedlars Arrested, *Gravesend & Northfleet Standard*, 24 June 1905 p.2

Brutal Crime in Kent, Mutilated Corpse Found in a Meadow, *Illustrated Police News*, 24 June 1905, p.7

Murder Mystery Village Tragedy Albanian Murdered in Field, *The People*, 25 June 1905, p.11

Albanian Mat Pedlars Death, *Belper News*, 27 June 1905 p.3

Tragedy at Tenterden, Foreigner Murdered, *Folkestone Express & Hythe Advertiser*, 28 June 1905 p.7

Nottingham Evening Post 30 June p 6

The Tenterden Tragedy, Prisoner Demeanour, *Kent Times*, 1 July 1905, p.8

South East Gazette 1 July 1905.

Kent Assizes, A Long List, *Gravesend Reporter*, 15 July 1905, p.2

Kent Times, 15 July 1905, p4.

South East Gazette, Saturday 15 July p 8

Tenterden Murder, Sentence of Death. *Kent Times* 15 July p4

The Tenterden Tragedy, Sentence of Death, *Folkestone Express*, 22 July 1905, p.6

The Tenterden Murder, Ben Ali Confession, *Faversham News*, 8 July 1905, p.8

Westminster Gazette 1 Aug 1905 p 6.

The Tenterden Murder, Algerian Executed, *East Anglian Times*, 2 August 1905, p.8

Moslems Execution, *Daily Mirror* 2 August page 5

Algerian Murderer Resigned To His Fate, *Diss Express*, 4 August 1905, p.7

Execution at Maidstone, *Kent and Sussex Courier*, 4 August. 1905, p10

The Tenterden Murder, Execution of Ben Ali, *Kent Times*, 5 August 1905.

The Tenterden Murder, Ben Ali Executed, Denial of clemency, *Faversham News,* 5 August 1905, p.3

East Kent Gazette 5 Aug 1905.

Don't miss out!

Visit the website below and you can sign up to receive emails whenever John Brookland publishes a new book. There's no charge and no obligation.

https://books2read.com/r/B-A-KTBAB-JBEKD

BOOKS 2 READ

Connecting independent readers to independent writers.

Also by John Brookland

The Edwardian Detective Edwin Fowle Series
The Tonbridge Murder, A Gruesome Murder That Shocked
Edwardian Society
The Tenterden Murder, An Edwardian Murder Most Brutal

Standalone
Cruelty In Paradise

Watch for more at https://www.bitzabooks.co.uk.

About the Author

John Brookland is now retired and lives in Suffolk, U.K. after a long-varied career working at the sharp end of animal welfare in the U.K and abroad. Having always had an interest in social history and true crime he now researches and writes books and magazine articles on these subjects. These include the Detective Edwin Fowle series chronicling the exploits of a real celebrated Edwardian detective. He has also authored memoirs of his work helping animals in the U.K. and abroad and books on the history of department stores and the War Horses.

He also authors a popular educational animal welfare blog *www.animalrightsandwrongs.uk* commentating on international and U.K. animal issues with readers in over 70 countries. When not writing he enjoys travelling with his partner Debbie to exotic places to view wildlife and wandering the U.K. countryside.

Read more at https://www.bitzabooks.co.uk.

Milton Keynes UK
Ingram Content Group UK Ltd.
UKHW020740281124
3218UKWH00021B/83

9 781068 645037